VICTORY

★ ★ ★ ★ ★ ★ ★ ★ ★ ★ ★ ★ ★

Advance Praise for VICTORY

It's not attraction; it's ACTION that powers your success. Broughton and Dyer blueprint how to achieve VICTORY on the business battlefield by tapping into your unconquerable warrior spirit.

—Darren Hardy
Publisher *SUCCESS* Magazine
Bestselling author, *The Compound Effect and Living Your Best Year Ever*

★ ★ ★ ★ ★

Larry Broughton is a great example of why veterans own businesses at twice the rate of non-veterans. The Army pushed him beyond limits he never knew he had that ambition spilled over into his civilian career as a Vetrepreneur®. Larry's a smart, tenacious business leader who honed his skills in service to his country. Let VICTORY inspire your business to new heights by bringing clarity of purpose, motivation to persevere and an inspiration to dream big.

—Chris Hale, President
National Veteran-Owned Business Association (NaVOBA)
Naval Academy Graduate
U.S. Navy Veteran
BuyVeteran.com

★ ★ ★ ★ ★

The hardest thing about business is everything; but it gets easier with VICTORY on your side.

—Rick Ferri, CFA
Founder/President of Portfolio Solutions
Maj, USMC (Ret) and Vetrepreneur® since 1999
Author of seven books, including *The Power of Passive Investing*
PortfolioSolutions.com

★ ★ ★ ★ ★

This powerful, action-oriented book is based on years of sustained entrepreneurial victories, by guys who have been there, and done that. Using Broughton & Dyer's business battle plan detailed in VICTORY, every entrepreneur can tap into their warrior spirit, and face the business battlefield with courage. Be warned: VICTORY is contagious.

—Brian Tracy

Speaker and author of *The Way to Wealth and Maximum Achievement*

BrianTracy.com

★ ★ ★ ★ ★

Entrepreneurs are too often distracted by the next big idea—the bright shiny object—and we loose focus and get off course. In business that can be frustrating and cost us a few dollars—in the military that slip-up can cost you your life. In VICTORY Larry & Phil share the lessons they learned in military service, and brilliantly chart the course to entrepreneurial success. These guys are the real deal—the new breed of warrior-entrepreneurs!

—Lisa Sasevich

Queen of Sales Conversion

LisaSasevich.com

★ ★ ★ ★ ★

In my work with hundreds of businesses, I have long admired the exceptional character and trustworthiness displayed by our Military Veterans. VICTORY provides this National Treasure (Veterans) with principles and practices that will accelerate business growth, job creation, and entrepreneurial success.

—Joe Calhoon, CSP

Business Strategist and Speaker

Author of *The 1-Hour Plan for Growth*

1Hour2Plan.com

★ ★ ★ ★ ★

VICTORY inspires, it motivates, and is that needed jump-start to take action towards entrepreneurial success! This fast-paced, no-nonsense road map gets you out of your head, and on your journey towards your potential. Larry and Phil are RockStars among entrepreneurs, and this book will show you all the backstage secrets to achieve RockStar status in your industry.

—Craig Duswalt
Professional Speaker and Author
Creator of the RockStar System for Success
CraigDuswalt.com

★ ★ ★ ★ ★

Finally! A no bull, take-no-prisoners approach to securing entrepreneurial success—by vets for vets. Broughton and Dyer served our country in military uniform, and they continue to do so as warriors in the Vetrepreneur® Revolution. VICTORY is a must read for any veteran who dreams of entrepreneurial success.

—Bill Rogin
President/Executive Producer of Rogin Entertainment
RoginEntertainment.com

★ ★ ★ ★ ★

Larry and Phil present a simple, yet provocative approach to entrepreneurial success: Action Is Power! Any business can find success if VICTORY is the only option.

—Tony Hsieh
Author of #1 NY Times Bestseller, *Delivering Happiness*
CEO, Zappos
Zappos.com

★ ★ ★ ★ ★

VICTORY brilliantly shows how that same warrior ethos that serves our military members in battle, serves our entrepreneur class in the business arena. It's often the simplest of ideas that are the most profound: take rapid, decisive action; make course corrections along the way; never surrender; and serve others. With VICTORY Broughton & Dyer become the vanguard of the Vetrepreneur Revolution.

—Chip Conley

Founder and Executive Chair, Joie de Vivre Hospitality

Author, *PEAK: How Great Companies Get Their Mojo from Maslow*

ChipConley.com

★　★　★　★　★

Teammates, it is an honor to introduce you to VICTORY, Larry Broughton and Phil Dyer's tested and true action plan of a book. Both are fellow vets, remarkable entrepreneurs, and men on a mission to help others defy the odds. I hope you find them as inspiring as I do.

I believe you'll find their message of "Continue Mission" aka CHARLIE MIKE, one that will help you to NEVER GIVE UP ON YOUR DREAMS! Would-be Vetrepreneurs®, VICTORY is a book that will help you unlock your dreams and make them a reality. Lock 'n Load!

—Alden Mills

Former Navy SEAL

CEO and Founder, Perfect Fitness

PerfectFitness.com

★　★　★　★　★

Victory is knocking at the door for anyone who applies the pragmatic lessons taught in Broughton and Dyer's VICTORY. This is not necessarily a book that people will read; it will more likely become a mission they embrace. Anyone longing for a successful life will benefit from this no nonsense, take-no-prisoners book! Read VICTORY today and WIN tomorrow!

—Dave Dias
Insurance Executive, Serial Entrepreneur
DaveDias.com

★ ★ ★ ★ ★

Broughton and Dyer are leading the victory charge in the entrepreneurial arena. Their mission is simple: stop dreaming and start doing! The challenge? Simple is not always easy. Use VICTORY to break through the roadblocks keeping you from achieving victory in your own life!

—Tom Antion
Founder Internet Marketing Training Center of Virginia
IMTCVA.org

★ ★ ★ ★ ★

Every entrepreneur knows it, every warrior lives it, and VICTORY reinforces it: inaction is worse than failure! This book captures the wisdom gained by sustained entrepreneurial victory, and the agony of business defeat. Do not venture on to the business battlefield alone…use VICTORY as your guide!

—Jonathan Sprinkles
Television analyst, Featured columnist
Former National Speaker of the Year
JSprinkles.com

★ ★ ★ ★ ★

As a former fighter pilot turned entrepreneur, I found VICTORY to be a hard-hitting, fast-paced, and to-the-point presentation on achieving success as a Veteran. Let's face it…Larry and Phil have been there, they've done that… and they are still doing it today. In my mind, they are the nation's leading "Top Guns" for showing people like us how to get more done, in less time, make more money, and take more time off. Get the book, read it…then read it again. It's just that good.

—Ed Rush
Former USMC F-18 Pilot
Speaker and Author of *Fighter Pilot Performance for Business*
EdRush.com

★ ★ ★ ★ ★

If you ever dreamed of entrepreneurial success, then read, absorb and use the strategies in this brilliant book by my friends Larry Broughton and Phil Dyer. What makes this book transformational and the #1 business book for military veteran entrepreneurs is that the ideas and concepts are taught by two military veteran entrepreneurs who have been there, done that and are still successfully doing it today! This is not textbook theory, but REAL-LIFE, in the trenches strategies THAT WORK! Larry and Phil are two business leaders with the highest integrity who are successful, heart-centered entrepreneurs who TRULY care about helping you. This book should be mandatory reading for all military veterans!

—James Malinchak
Featured on ABC's Hit TV Show, "Secret Millionaire"
Founder, BigMoneySpeaker.com

★ ★ ★ ★ ★

This is a business book that's fun to read, easy to comprehend, simple to apply, and inspires action! You don't have to be a Veteran of the Armed Forces to enjoy this book and benefit from the seven principles Larry and Phil have laid out, but for those of us who are, we've now got what we've been looking for—concrete direction from guys just like us.

—Darrell Fusaro
Cartoonist
Veteran, United States Coast Guard
Producer of the Emmy® nominated LOCAL EDITION
DarrellFusaro.com

★ ★ ★ ★ ★

The essentials of winning in business are the essentials of winning in combat. The VICTORY approach is based on mission-tested disciplines of robust preparation, trust, duty, and commitment; the elements that build an effective leader. You will not succeed without good planning, but you will not succeed merely because you plan. It will take the courage and heart of a warrior. This book will equip the leader who will ultimately go into the fray enabling the followers to experience greatness. Enjoy VICTORY...may it be yours as well.

—Jeff Abbott
Consultant, Chairperson at Convene
Veteran, United States Army
TheAbbottWay.com

★ ★ ★ ★ ★

VICTORY

★ ★ ★ ★ ★ ★ ★ ★ ★ ★ ★ ★ ★ ★

7 Entrepreneur Success
Strategies for Veterans

LARRY BROUGHTON

Former Special Forces Operator, Ernst & Young Entrepreneur of the Year®
and NaVOBA's Vetrepreneur® of the Year

PHIL DYER, CFP®, RLP®, CPCC

West Point Graduate and America's Entrepreneur Strategist™

BANDERA
—PUBLISHING—

Acknowledgements

This book has been swirling around in our imaginations for several years, but it wasn't until the sparks began to fly during a brainstorming session at Phil's office, just outside of Baltimore, MD, on October 26th, 2010 that it all came together. There's no better feeling in the business world than collaborating on a project with partners and teammates who are in simpatico, who share a heart for serving others, the drive to make a difference, and the determination to get things done. That's how things have been with the development of the VICTORY Success System and our first book together, VICTORY: 7 Entrepreneur Success Strategies for Veterans.

The ideas, concepts and writings are ours, based on years of trial and error in the Vetrepreneur® arena. The completion of this book project, however, would not have been possible without the help and support of dozens of people around us who believe in us, and the value of this book's message. Frankly, we've been in awe at the number of late hours our editors, graphic artists, and formatting team have been willing to work on this project so we could quickly get the ideas out of our heads, on to paper/hard drive, through the printing process, and in to book stores. We continue to be surprised and humbled by the growing support among our fellow military veteran entrepreneurs who have committed to join us, the vanguard, of what we're calling the Vetrepreneur® Revolution.

Thanks from Larry & Phil:

Very special thanks go out to two amazing teams without which this book would never have come together: First, to Cindy Tyler and Team Vervante for their cover design and book formatting/layout work. Second, to Peggy Murrah and her PMA team for their last minute (and we do mean LAST minute) copy editing support. Both of these amazing teams worked heroically on ridiculously tight time lines and delivered magnificently.

Linda Schenk, Petra Boucher and U.S. Air Force vet Steven Deaton for creating our supporting website and managing a myriad of technical details. Petra was also instrumental in managing the recording and transcription process that formed the basis of the book.

Personal branding gurus James Malinchak and Craig Duswalt, who both pushed us to get our unique ideas into book format. We are blessed by their ongoing support for us, and their belief in our cause.

Dorit Theis and her photography team for our publicity photos.

To our friend Laurie Baker, for her unwavering support and encouragement for our mission, for opening doors that seem out of reach, and for her heart for our warriors.

To fellow Vetrepreneur® Chris Hale, and the entire team at NaVOBA (who hold the registered trademark for the term "Vetrepreneur®") for their tireless support and advocacy on behalf of the military veteran entrepreneur and the Buy Veteran® movements.

To all those who chose the warrior lifestyle and serve(d) our country in uniform; and to the Vetrepreneurs® who now serve on the business battlefield.

Personal Thanks from Larry Broughton:

My deepest gratitude goes out to the following: my stunning bride, Suzanne, for believing in me, and encouraging me during the ups and downs of the entrepreneurial lifestyle; Emily and Ben, who see me at my goofiest, and still yell, "Daddy" when I walk in the door at night; my brother-Vetrepreneur® and co-author Phil Dyer, for his constant encouragement and uncanny way of taking complex ideas and bringing clarity, he epitomizes the term "rapid action;" marketing genius Donny Deutsch who encouraged me to get my thoughts into book form; personal development guru, and Publisher of SUCCESS Magazine Darren Hardy who reminded me of the power of short, encouraging emails when he sent me the simple message, "Bravo! Damn, always GREAT stuff," referring to my weekly FLASHPOINTS…the timing was perfect; Jeff Abbott and members of Convene Group 6 for the great coaching, friendship and stellar mastermind sessions; my SF brothers at 10th and 12th Special Groups, particularly the guys at ODA 064 and ODA 1275; all our military service members and veterans who have dared to pick up the sword and shield to serve a cause greater than themselves; my rock star assistant Shawna Shope who has gone above and beyond the call of duty to get this project off the ground, while simultaneously running the office at Broughton Hotels; my older brother Bryan, who in his dying showed me that life is too short not to follow your dreams; my twin brother Barry for being one of my heroes, and showing me that we must follow our passions, even if it means changing directions; and the executive corral of stallions at Broughton Hotels who seem to tolerate me and keep the organization on track when I'm distracted with crazy entrepreneurial adventures: Robert Rycroft, Steve Buckler, Stephen Medel, and especially Jim Sichta—the best business partner I could ever ask for; and God for giving me another chance (again and again), for His grace, and speaking words of love and encouragement through my inner voice.

Special thanks to all those folks who "encouraged" me to turn back and stay in the calm waters, and told me that it was scary out there past the horizon.

Personal Thanks from Phil Dyer:

I am so very, very thankful to the people whose unflagging encouragement made this book possible: my wife Kerry, for her unwavering support and standing by *me through the twists, turns and loops that embody serial entrepreneurship - she endured many late nights, early mornings and even the occasional panic attack during the final stages of this project; my son and daughter, who were always there with a hug or smile at just the right time; My amazing co-author, superb role-model and fellow Vetrepreneur®, Larry Broughton, for his unparalleled work ethic, seemingly effortless ability to connect with exactly the right people at the right time and his uncompromising belief in servant-leadership; Marilyn Dyer Blair, my recently retired mom who blazed the entrepreneurial trail that I chose to follow, and whose courage in the face of adversity is a true triumph; my brothers and sisters-in-arms from my West Point days to the present who have stood many lonely watches on distant shores far from home, especially those that have given the last full measure; Andrew, my Marine Recon brother who represents the best of the generation now coming of age; fellow personal development leader Jessica Eaves Mathews for her keen insight and sage advice; Sue Hoppin, my friend and colleague for being an incredible connecter with key centers of influence and always watching my six; Fabienne Fredrickson, whose butt-kicking admonition for me to "quit playing small" came at the perfect moment; to all of the mastermind partners from "Team Mitch" that supported this project from its birth; my clients, who have so honored me by allowing me to support them in taking their businesses—and lives—to new heights while doing what I absolutely love; finally, the Creator for gracing me with my unique gifts and imbuing me with a heart of service.*

TABLE OF CONTENTS

FOREWORD

★ ★ ★ ★ ★ ★ ★ ★ ★ ★ ★ ★ ★ ★ ★ ★ ★ ★ ★

I've spent my entire adult life as a warrior. I graduated from West Point, served as a military intelligence officer in the Army, completed Airborne school and Ranger training, battled wits with some of the brightest minds in the country while obtaining my law degree and M.B.A. at UCLA, and I've slugged it out with the best of them in the entrepreneurial arena.

More than a decade after leaving active military duty I went through a sixteen week, very public interview process on Donald Trump's wildly popular show *The Apprentice: Season 2*. After being chosen by Mr. Trump to serve by his side, everywhere I went I was asked by friends, business associates, strangers and media if my military background had helped me win *The Apprentice*. The answer was always an unqualified yes.

The more I was asked about it, the more I realized that my time in uniform was the very foundation for how I live my life and run my businesses. It was during that time that I learned, I lead, and I served. It was there I came to understand the importance of solid character, including integrity, duty, and loyalty—it was there I recognized the value of perseverance, planning and teamwork.

I had been asked so many times about how my military service had served me in being chosen as Mr. Trump's Apprentice, that I wrote a book called *Take Command: 10 Leadership Principles I Learned In The*

1

Military And Put To Work For Donald Trump. You have my word that when you apply the principles described in my book to your business life, you'll gain that competitive edge needed to succeed.

I love what Larry Broughton and Phil Dyer have created with their book, *VICTORY*. The mission-tested entrepreneurial strategies in this book will supercharge your business and propel you to success. Larry and Phil are not regurgitating business theory; they're sharing tried and true, action-oriented principles they've used themselves and have learned from interviewing other successful military veteran entrepreneurs (including me). Given my own experience, it doesn't surprise me, as pointed out in this book, that military veterans have the makings of exceptional entrepreneurs, and have the opportunity to fill the leadership void in our country's business community. After reading this book, I hope you'll join us.

Although many have come to know me from my life as *The Apprentice*, life outside the Trump Organization has been just as exciting, challenging and rewarding. I've experienced significant success building and managing forward-thinking and innovative emerging brands, including my current company, Fastpoint Games (formerly Rotohog), which has become one of the leaders in fantasy and traditional game platforms for brands ranging from Turner Sports, Disney/ABC, and NASCAR. The success I'm most proud of, however, is the life I've built with my beautiful family. Without them, my life would not be complete.

Ok, now stop dreaming, and start doing. Take action by applying the principles and strategies from VICTORY, and grab the greatness you deserve.

—Kelly Perdew

CEO, Fastpoint Games; Winner, Donald Trump's *The Apprentice 2;* Author, *Take Command*; West Point Graduate (1989); KellyPerdew.com

INTRODUCTION

★ ★ ★ ★ ★ ★ ★ ★ ★ ★ ★ ★ ★ ★ ★ ★ ★ ★ ★ ★

STOP! READ THIS FIRST!

"Lock 'n load! We're moving out." That phrase will grab any veteran's attention and start the adrenaline pumping. It's brief. It's descriptive. And when we hear it, we know it's time for action. In similar fashion, we're committed to the same approach in addressing the issues faced by current and aspiring Military Veteran Entrepreneurs, because, frankly, we're pissed-off! We're sick and tired of seeing our veteran brothers and sisters led down the wrong path, wasting time, wasting money, and getting frustrated as they try to launch their dream of entrepreneurship.

Here's what you can expect from us in this book: straight talk, no bullsh★★, and an action-oriented approach to help propel you and your business towards significance and success.

We've written this book for you, a very special group of people, a group that we are proud to be a part of! The group? Military veterans and retirees who have decided to start their own business. Some call us Vetrepreneurs®, but we're also known as Military Veteran Entrepreneurs, or MVEs. As a whole, we are a dedicated and tenacious bunch. We start businesses at a rate 4 times higher than the general population and many of today's most innovate and successful business leaders come from military backgrounds. And we are strong, with 1

3

in 7 veteran-owned businesses accounting for an estimated 3 million (14 percent) of all small businesses in the United States today.

Sure, the government does its best to help MVEs. We've audited many of the programs available through installation transition offices, the Veterans Administration (VA) and the Small Business Administration designed to support veterans who possess the entrepreneurial spirit. Quite frankly, we're unimpressed. While some innovative initiatives exist, many of these well-intentioned programs are only marginally successful in helping MVEs start, run and grow their businesses

So why aren't these programs more successful? Most of the people who run and administer these programs are genuinely trying to help. Unfortunately, many of the people that dream up these programs, teach these programs and make key decisions on these programs have _never_ actually started or run a successful business. They have no first-hand knowledge of the unique challenges that come with entrepreneurship, nor the practical experience in the marketing, team-building and growth strategies that are critical for achieving sustainable success in today's rapidly changing business world. Finally, very few of them share the unique combination of discipline, drive and "make it happen" attitude that makes so many MVEs great entrepreneurs.

We strongly believe that today's MVEs need more than rote formulas, generic advice and one-size-fits-all governmental solutions. They need a customizable battle plan of specific success strategies that apply to a business of any size: from a one-person operation or a small ensemble firm to a national (or international) multi-site company that is being built for eventual sale or to go public.

In this book, we present the success strategies you need in order to build and grow your business. These are strategies that we have used in our combined 60 years of entrepreneurial and leadership experience, as well as what we have learned from interviewing, mentoring, and coaching dozens of high-achieving MVEs over the last 5 years.

These strategies will help you achieve financial success with your business, and empower you to create an organization that is a reflection of your individual passion, brilliance, unique skills and core values. We will show you how to connect with your ideal clients and support your family, community, and the broader world.

Keep in mind that these are not simply our *theories* concerning what *might* work in business. These are field-tested, practical ideas that anyone can use to improve his or her business. Maybe you are an aspiring MVE who has passion and an idea. Or, you're an MVE who has been in business for a couple of years, but you've gotten "bogged down" in the sea of conflicting priorities that always arise as a business grows. You may even be a highly successful MVE that is looking for 1 or 2 tips or "secret weapons" you can use to elevate your business to the next level.

Wherever you find yourself, you will find something in this book that will help you. We GUARANTEE it! If after reading this book, and implementing the success strategies described herein, you don't find your business in better condition and heading for significant growth, let us know. Tell us we're full of crap and we'll refund the money you paid for this book! Sounds fair, doesn't it?

At this point, you might be asking yourself, "Why should I believe you guys? How do you guys know what makes for a successful MVE?" Those are good questions. So, here's the deal:

Who Are We?

We are Larry Broughton and Phil Dyer. As we shared earlier, we have over 60 years of combined entrepreneurial and leadership experience…real-world experience…not just classroom theory. We have celebrated the thrill of business victories and dealt with the agony of business defeats. We understand the tremendous value of actually making mistakes in business, learning from them, correcting course and NOT repeating those same mistakes.

Most importantly, we have been exactly where you are right now, whether you are facing the simultaneous excitement and fear of starting your first business or are up and running but facing daunting obstacles on growing your business or are ready to "go national" and beyond. Please allow us to share a bit more about our backgrounds and how best to use this book and then we will dive right in!

★ ★ ★ ★ ★ ★ ★ ★ ★ ★ ★ ★ ★ ★ ★ ★ ★

Larry's Story

"I spent nearly 8 years on Special Forces A-Teams (commonly known as the Green Berets) in the U.S. Army, where I traveled the world, and attained the rank of Staff Sergeant. I then took the lessons I learned there and applied them to the business world. I'm a serial entrepreneur; have bought and sold several businesses; and am the founder and CEO of Broughton Hospitality, a nationally known, multi-unit, award-winning company which is considered a leader in the boutique hotel industry.

I've been privileged to receive several business awards, including Ernst & Young's Entrepreneur of the Year Award®. The National Veteran-Owned Business Association named me their Vetrepreneur® of the Year, and Entrepreneur Magazine included Broughton Hospitality on their Hot 500 List of Fastest Growing Privately Held Companies.

I've also authored several articles and books on leadership, team building and entrepreneurial significance (and speak to national audiences on these topics), and have been featured in newspaper and magazine articles across the country. I've been honored to be a guest on news and TV programs on every major network, and I'm living an absolutely blessed life!"

Phil's Story

"I graduated from the United States Military Academy at West Point in 1985 and served on active duty as an Armor officer for 5 years. After separating from active service as an Army Captain, I enjoyed highly successful "duty assignments" in corporate sales for a Fortune 50 company and as a fee-only financial planner.

Over the last 15 years, I have advised hundreds of entrepreneurs on financial, tax and success strategies to effectively build their businesses during both up and down markets. I have given nearly 700 speeches to small business, corporate, non-profit and governmental audiences on a variety of financial and business topics and have shared the stage with some of today's most innovative business thought leaders. I enjoy writing, with over 100 business/financial by-lines and am frequently quoted on business and financial topics by Money, Kiplinger's, Men's Health and numerous other publications.

As a serial entrepreneur, I have started, run and sold two small businesses and currently actively own a boutique financial planning firm, as well as a strategic business consulting company. I recently had the good fortune to be chosen as the MVC (Most Valuable Contributor) by 300 small business peers for my innovations in marketing and business building."

The principles in this book are the ones that we have personally used to create, operate and grow several successful businesses. They are also tested and confirmed by other MVEs and successful entrepreneurs from around the country. We are convinced they can help you do the same!

How This Book is Organized

We've constructed this book with three goals in mind:

★ To give you concise information with a minimal amount of fluff.
★ To provide relevant examples of the principles in the book from the lives of fellow MVEs who have achieved high levels of success.
★ Empower you to take positive action right away.

Each chapter title identifies a mission-tested success strategy that spells the acrostic "V.I.C.T.O.R.Y."

V	Vision
I	Intel
C	Coaching
T	Team
O	Ops
R	Rapid Action
Y	You

Each chapter contains:

★ **Key Challenge**: We have had the good fortune to interview, mentor/coach, mastermind with and learn from hundreds of other entrepreneurs. From these experiences, we have distilled down 7 key challenges that most MVEs face at various times in starting and growing their business.

★ **Success Strategy**: The titles of Chapters 1 through 7 describe the mission-tested solutions based on real-world experience—not theory—for dealing with each key challenge. **Developing Your VICTORY Success Plan (Chapter 8)** provides a step-by-step formula to create your VICTORY Success Battle Plan, regardless of the current stage of your business.

★ **Intel Insights**: These short sidebars contain critical tips for identifying and navigating the business minefields that obstruct, delay or adversely redirect even the most experienced MVEs.

★ **Million Dollar Minute Exercise**: Some of you may recall the live-fire public relations firepower demonstrations that were more common in years past. In the Army, we called these million dollar minutes, since upwards of $1 million of ordinance could easily be expended during a fairly short time. In our book, the **Million Dollar Minute** takes on a different meaning. They are short, focus exercises designed to more fully connect you with the key strategies of Vision, Intel, Coaching, Team, Ops, Rapid Action and You. While some of the exercises definitely take more than a minute to complete and we won't guarantee that any of them will put $1 million directly in your pocket, they are specifically designed to help you step back, get a clear sight picture on your business and your own internal strengths and take positive action.

How To Use This Book

If You are an Aspiring MVE or in Start-up Mode

Read the book cover to cover without skipping around. Complete the **Million Dollar Minute** exercises and assessments that we recommend. Then, continue on to the companion website for more information (**www.VictorySuccessResources.com**). This will help give you the 360° perspective and the 30,000 foot view that is often lost when you are in the middle of starting and building your business.

Also, carefully review the **Resources** and **Learn More** chapters of this book. This will enable you to take full advantage of the powerful tools and support systems available for today's forward-thinking MVE.

If You are Already Running a Successful Business

If you have hit a roadblock or gotten bogged down in business quicksand, you may want to use this book differently. Skim the book and zero in on the success strategies that really speak to you. Explore them fully and take action.

In our experience, current business owners tend to become stuck in a few key areas, and find themselves too close to their own situation to clearly diagnose what they should do next. If this is you, think of this book as a toolkit: reach into it for the proper tool to take course corrective action, so that your business starts firing on all cylinders.

Before You Get Started

We are excited about the principles that you will find in this book. We know they are going to help you take your business to a new level.

But before you begin reading, we want you to take a very important first step. This is not required, but if you are as committed to the success of your business as we are, you'll find our suggestion to be absolutely essential.

We believe that MVEs are most successful when they understand themselves, as well as their businesses. For that reason, we want you to use a couple of the most powerful assessment tools we have found to help you better understand who you are, and the strengths you possess.

StrengthsFinder 2.0 is a book (and an online assessment tool) that will help you uncover your 5 inherent strengths. Many of us spend too much time doing things we are not naturally gifted to do. *StrengthsFinder 2.0* will help you connect to your talents, so that you can invest your time and energy doing what you do best. If you don't want to read the entire book, take the online assessment, and then just read the five chapters that relate to your strengths.

The *Kolbe A Index* is an online assessment tool that will show you how you naturally operate in a given situation. It will also show you how you can use your innate Method of Operation in order to be more productive. The better you understand what you do best, the more you can operate effectively out of your strengths.

These assessments don't take long to complete, and the knowledge you will gain about yourself will be invaluable as you apply the principles in this book to your business. Invest the time to do them right now! You can find links to both the *Kolbe A Index* and *StrengthsFinders 2.0* on the **Resources** page at this book's website (**www.VictorySuccessResources.com**).

Once you have completed these assessments, you are ready to dive into the VICTORY principles in this book. Let's get started!

VISION

★ ★ ★ ★ ★ ★ ★ ★ ★ ★ ★ ★ ★ ★ ★ ★ ★ ★ ★

Without vision, the people will perish.
—Proverbs 29:18

The soul becomes dyed with the color of its thoughts.
—Marcus Aurelius

Key Challenge

Many Military Veteran Entrepreneurs lack a clear vision of what they (and their companies) are truly capable of. They don't yet realize the positive impact they can have on their families, clients/customers and broader communities. The reason? They haven't connected with their unique strengths and abilities, their core values and their guiding principles—the very things that form the foundation of sustainable success—to craft a guiding vision for both personal and business success. **You won't get far without a clear vision!**

In this chapter, we stress the importance of having a clear vision for your business, a vision grounded in your core principles. Now it may surprise you to learn that you can operate a reasonably successful business without a clear vision. Every day, we use products and services provided by companies that don't have a vision statement.

You can absolutely achieve a certain level of success in business without a vision for your organization, but it will be very difficult to successfully navigate the turbulent waters of economic downturns, sustainable business growth, or key personnel changes without a clearly articulated vision.

There is no more important strategy to attain enduring success than vision

If you want to build an exceptional organization, one that moves from good to great, you MUST have a clearly stated vision to guide you. Our experience, and the experience of the MVEs we've studied, shows us that wildly successful organizations share several common characteristics. Chief among them is a clear vision of where they are going and what success means for them.

Let's be crystal clear about this: there's no more important strategy to attain enduring success than vision. Long-term, sustainable success will evade you, unless you possess a clear vision of where you're going as an organization, and as a person.

Why is vision so important? It allows you as a leader to effectively communicate your ideas, goals and aspirations. We're not just talking about physical, tangible goals here. It also includes your core values—those foundational principles in your life that guide everything you do. Vision keeps you going in the right direction, even when you are facing the trials and tribulations that entrepreneurs go through at every level of business.

One of Larry's favorite sayings from his martial arts training is "Only those who can see the invisible can do the impossible."

A vision helps you see the invisible—it helps you see what's possible. When you run your business—or your life, for that matter—without a vision or mission statement, it's like making contact with the enemy without a battle plan or an operations order.

One of the quotes from the beginning of this chapter (Proverbs 29:18) states, "Without vision, the people will perish." We have found that too many entrepreneurs don't understand the truth of this. They devalue the importance of vision. It's their loss—they lose out on the sense of direction vision provides for the leader, and for his team.

Without vision, your business is likely to veer off course when troubles hit. If you maintain your vision, it allows you to steer through those difficult times. You have that beacon of vision ahead of you, guiding you in the right direction. If you don't have that, you're going to wander all over the place, looking for solutions and answers. You might try one thing today, and another thing tomorrow, with nothing really coming together.

We have made virtually every mistake that you can possibly make in business. (In fact, we believe that in order to achieve success, you need to make a lot of mistakes!) One of the most important parts of having a crystal-clear vision is that when you *do* make a mistake, your vision gets you back on track.

Particularly in difficult economic times, it's easy to chase after the quick-fix or silver bullet that will make everything OK. For instance, when revenue starts to slide, or you are having challenges with your personnel, you need to know what's important to you. You need to know where you want your business to go. Otherwise, you may find yourself going for the quick-fix, cutting corners or even compromising your ethics "just this one time" to get things back on track.

With a clear vision, when you hit a rough patch, you won't end up spinning out of control, hoping to find your way. You can get back to where you need to be, without wasting time. When you have that vision in front of you, it guides you back to what's essential to your business.

You can ask yourself the important question: What am I trying to achieve? Then you can take the necessary steps in order to move forward in the right direction.

Vision also provides you with the fuel you need to move forward. A clearly defined vision motivates you to keep going. When you have what James Collins and Jerry Porras, authors of *Built to Last*, call a "big, hairy, audacious goal," a goal of really making a difference in the world with your business, the vision itself creates movement.

A clear vision becomes your battle cry, your call to action

Clear vision has provided the motivation for the great advances of history. For example, if you look at the great explorers—Columbus, Magellan, Lewis and Clark—they each had a vision of what could be; they had a vision of what they could accomplish. They fantasized about what was beyond the horizon. That vision propelled them forward into the unknown. As an entrepreneur, you are like those explorers: you must have a vision of what the future can be.

A clear vision becomes your battle cry, your call to action. This kind of vision can inspire team members to give their best. It ignites creativity. It allows you to attract the best people—the "rock stars" of your industry—because being part of something bigger than yourself is a prime motivator for many top performers. It helps you connect with the customers that are going to be most loyal to your company—the ones that will become your raving fans. In the next two key items, we'll look at how your vision affects your employees and customers, as well as how to discover your vision for your business.

Here are the vision statements of a few well-known companies... note how simple some are:

★ **Apple Vision Statement:** Apple is committed to bringing the best personal computing experience to students, educators, creative professionals and consumers around the world through its innovative hardware, software, and internet offerings.

★ **Google Vision Statement:** To develop a perfect search engine.

★ **Coca-Cola Vision Statement:** To achieve sustainable growth, we have established a vision with clear goals:

  ★ Profit: Maximizing return to share owners while being mindful of our overall responsibilities.

  ★ People: Being a great place to work where people are inspired to be the best they can be.

  ★ Portfolio: Bringing to the world a portfolio of beverage brands that anticipate and satisfy people's desires and needs.

  ★ Partners: Nurturing a winning network of partners and building mutual loyalty.

  ★ Planet: Being a responsible global citizen that makes a difference.

Your ability to communicate a clear vision will dramatically affect your business

Exceptional organizations always have vision statements. Leaders of these organizations know that these statements must be clear, and they must be effectively communicated to their team members. By team members, we mean all the stakeholders in the business: investors, vendors, team members (employees), and even clients/customers. You need all the people who are essential to your company's success to buy into your vision.

When you effectively communicate your vision, it keeps your team members inspired. It helps them make decisions. We hear the same complaints from too many entrepreneurs: they have a difficult time managing their teams. Team members keep interrupting them, asking the same questions over and over again. They're afraid to make decisions by themselves.

When we hear about situations like this, it's a sign that there is a problem with the leader communicating the company's vision. It's usually the case that the team members don't know what the vision is for the organization. In organizations where every person understands the vision—both the core values and the hard, tangible goals— team members are able to make effective decisions by themselves. The company's vision helps them navigate, even when they are in uncharted waters.

Intel Insight

Clearly Communicating Your Vision
Attracts Great Employees!
Larry Broughton
Founder/CEO of Broughton Hospitality Group

I found this to be true in my company, Broughton Hospitality. I started my company with a clearly defined vision, and I was able to articulate that vision clearly. That gave me the ability to attract top-notch hospitality people to work with me.

In the early days of our organization, I was able to hire industry rock stars who could have worked anywhere they chose. Some of my new team members were asked by friends and industry colleagues "Why are you working for this Brougton guy? He's only got 2 small hotels! You should be a COO or CFO someplace else!" The reason I could hire such great people was that they bought into my vision of growing an extraordinary organization far beyond our current stage. They knew I wanted to build a world-class hospitality organization that was based on innovation and accessibility, and a work environment that embraced honesty and integrity. My vision resonated with them. They got it, and wanted to change the industry with me.

When you are able to clearly communicate your vision, you will be able to connect with your customers on a deeper level. In fact, you may end up creating customers who are also huge fans of your business. A great example of this is Apple, Inc. They stayed true to their vision, even though for decades they lagged behind their competition in terms of worldwide market share in the PC and mobile device industry.

Their vision was to provide a very user-friendly interface. They built products that were simple enough for anyone to use, even without a degree in technology. Staying true to that vision has definitely paid off. If you look at Apple over the last 5 to 7 years, they've made huge strides by pulling traditional business users into the Mac universe, and creating devices that people love and adore.

They kept pursuing their vision to make devices that people love for their functionality and ease of use. As a result, they developed a fiercely loyal consumer base—the kind of customers that will save an organization during difficult times. The rest of the computer industry is playing catch-up.

Have you ever been to Apple store? It's always packed, regardless of the time of day. The stores aren't much to look at, yet people flock there to spend their money on Apple products, get hands-on training from knowledgeable trainers and learn to make the most of their technology purchase. By contrast, other computer companies such as Dell and Gateway, opened retail stores with little success. The stores were usually empty, poorly staffed and ultimately abandoned for a multi-line reseller model.

What set Apple apart? Their customers bought into the company's vision and they are very loyal. In fact, team members there don't really need to push for sales. They simply help people out: they provide information, answer questions, demo products, and empower people to make decisions.

Chick-fil-A, founded by WWII U.S. Army veteran Truett Cathy, is another example of a company that is attracting both customers and team members because of its vision. They have a waiting list of people who want to be operator/partners with them because people understand and subscribe to the vision. Even before they begin working for the organization, they know they want to work for Chick-fil-A because of the values the company has defined.

By having a clearly defined vision, Chick-fil-A attracts leading entrepreneurs and food industry people up and down the corporate ladder. The company puts a high priority on its people having quality time with their families, so Chick-fil-A goes against the grain. Every other quick-service restaurant is open on Sundays. Chick-fil-A restaurants are always closed Sundays. But because they've attracted team members and customers who buy into the organization's vision, they produce more revenue on a per-unit basis in 6 days than anyone else does in 7 days.

So, we've seen that a clear vision can give your company guidance and motivation. It can help you attract the top people in your industry. Plus, it can help you build a rabidly loyal customer base. But, how do you discover your compelling vision, and communicate it effectively? We will answer those questions in the next section...

You Must Be Clear And Passionate In Communicating Your Vision

Remember, we are talking about creating a vision for your business. We find that many MVEs have a clear personal vision for their lives, but they haven't developed a clear vision for their businesses. You need to have a separate vision that applies specifically and directly to your company. Even though your personal values and core beliefs will be a big part of your company, you need a corporate vision that attracts and motivates your team members, and propels your business to a new level.

Creating a clear vision for your business can seem like a daunting task. The reality is that you will need to put in some time and brainpower to develop a vision. Sound a bit overwhelming? Don't worry! Just make sure you take the time to complete the **Million-Dollar Minute** exercise at the end of this chapter.

Your vision doesn't need to be complicated or earth shattering. In fact, the simpler it is, the more compelling it can be.

★ ★ ★ ★ ★ ★ ★ ★ ★ ★ ★ ★ ★ ★ ★ ★

Intel Insight:

What about the "Accidental Entrepreneur?"

What is an accidental entrepreneur? It's someone who doesn't begin with a clear vision of where they want to take their company. They don't know who they are, who they want to serve, or where they want to go. In many cases, they just decided they could do things better, and took the opportunity to start a business. They just dove in and started without taking the time to develop a vision for their business.

Maybe this describes you. You've had some success. You're comfortable from a personal income standpoint, but you're feeling restless—like something in your business is not quite right. You know you could be doing much more.

We know a **lot** of MVEs who are in this position and if this is where you are, let us repeat the timeless wisdom of Michael E. Gerber, author of the *E-Myth* and *E-Myth Revisited*: it's time to work ON your business for a bit, and not just IN your business!

Vision statements aren't just for big-shot leaders; they are for every leader, and every business. Go through the process of developing your vision that we talk about in this chapter. You will be glad you did!

You might want to create a mental movie of your company's future success. When the going gets tough and you're feeling discouraged, play the movie in your mind to remind yourself of where you are going. This will help you refocus on how good the rewards will feel once your company accomplishes them. Some strategic coaches even suggest you create a physical vision board or short movie to capture the essence of the vision you have for both yourself and your company and have them where you can see them every single day to keep the vision front and center.

You will need to revisit this process several times, until you create a vision you can commit to pursuing. Although your vision should be one that stretches and inspires your company to higher heights, it should be realistic. If you develop a vision that is too idealistic or overly optimistic, it is guaranteed that your team members will become frustrated. Be certain it's a vision that people will be proud to be part of, either as a team member or as a customer.

Be crystal clear, be authentic and unapologetic

Your vision needs to represent your core values in a very direct way. It's important for your vision to be crystal clear, to be authentic and unapologetic. You don't want to be confrontational—you just want to say, "This is who we are, this is what we believe in, and this is why. If that sounds good to you, we would love to do business with you. If you don't resonate with it, that's great. There are hundreds or thousands of other businesses out there with which you could be happy. But this is who we are—this is how we roll."

Once you have developed a vision that you, your team members and your customers want to take ownership of, it's time to communicate it. You want people to understand it, see the possibilities in it and themselves as part of it. In order for that to happen, you must be clear about what the vision is. Rehearse it in your head. Think about it often. When you are sure you have a clear picture of the vision, you will be able to share it with others.

The key to communicating your vision to others is to make sure it is communicated clearly and repeatedly. For most of the entrepreneurs we know, the most effective way to communicate vision is verbally. Talk about your vision with everyone you do business with—team members, vendors, customers, anyone—so that everyone understands who you are, and what your company is about.

Consider different ways to keep your vision in front of you and your team members, such as hanging a copy of your vision statement on the walls at work, putting it in a prominent spot on your website and featuring it prominently on your letterhead. The truth is that the more often you repeat it, the more ingrained it becomes in everyone's thinking.

Why do you need to repeat your vision often? You repeat it often because when you are in the trenches dealing with the day-to-day business "firefights"—dealing with vendors, dealing with production people, dealing with customers—it's easy to lose sight of why you are in business (for both you and your team members).

When you communicate your vision often, it reminds everybody: "Hey, this is why we do this. This is why we get out of bed every day."

Intel Insight:

Vision Statements from Fellow Vetrepreneurs

★ *To bring inspiration and innovation to every athlete in the world* -Nike (founded by Vetrepreneur Phil Knight)

★ *To be one of the world's most innovative full-service hospitality management and development companies by inspiring significance and distinction for our guests, associates and communities* -Broughton Hospitality Group (Founded by Vetrepreneur Larry Broughton)

★ *Creating solutions to enable consumers of all fitness levels to unlock their body's potential* -Perfect Fitness (Founded by Vetrepreneur Alden Mills)

★ *Our absolutely, positively spirit puts our customers at the heart of everything we do* -FedEx Service Statement (Founded by Vetrepreneur Fred Smith)

How will the vision for your company inspire, challenge and motivate?

People want and need something to aspire to. They want to be part of something greater than themselves. When you present your team members with a vision of the great things that the team can accomplish together, you give them a chance to be part of something bigger. This will be especially attractive to high achievers, who love to be challenged.

Wars are won by troops which have a strong will for victory,
clear goals before them, high moral standards, and devotion to
the banner under which they will go into battle.
—*Marshal Georgi Zhukov*

Million Dollar Minute

Stop Reading Right Now! Take some time right now to begin the process of developing a vision for your business. Don't rush it...this is a critical component for enduring success.

Here's a simple process that you can use to help you develop your company's vision. Begin by spending about thirty uninterrupted minutes alone. Find a secluded spot to slow your mind, reflect and then, think. Think about who you are, and what's important to you as the leader of this company. Think about the things you would like to see your business accomplish in the years ahead. (It's helpful to think about what you want to see your company do in the next 1, 3, 5 and 10 years and beyond.)

Don't be too critical of yourself at this early stage of the process. You'll very likely need to come back to revisit this process several times before you're content that you have adequately captured a vision for what it means for your business to be successful.

While you're reflecting, jot down some notes, phrases, and adjectives that come to mind. Imagine what success, and life, feels like once your company has accomplished its goals. Visualizing images of completed goals, and tapping in to their associated emotions, holds tremendous power.

If you get really stuck, ask yourself these important questions:

★ How many people can I help when I achieve my vision?
★ Who will receive a benefit when I achieve my vision?
★ What will the positive impact on my life be when I achieve my vision?

If you need some additional help in creating (or revising) your Vision statement, please visit our website at **www.VictorySuccessResources. com** and listen to our Vision Creation audio for more tips!

INTEL

★ ★ ★ ★ ★ ★ ★ ★ ★ ★ ★ ★ ★ ★ ★ ★ ★ ★ ★

Victorious warriors win first and then go to war,
while defeated warriors go to war first and then seek to win.
—Sun Tzu

Key Challenge

A surefire way to lose on the battlefield is to charge into battle without enough intel to make informed decisions. The same thing is true in business. Too many Military Veteran Entrepreneurs launch their business with incomplete intel on key areas that are essential for short and long-term success. Critical touch points include: knowledge on the market for their product/service, potential competition and the resources available to them.

Most importantly, many of them lack understanding of their most important assets: their own strengths and weaknesses!

One should know one's enemies, their alliances, their resources,
and the nature of their country, in order to plan a campaign.
—Frederick the Great

You Will Not Achieve Your Vision
Unless You Obtain Proper Intel

How important is intel in the military? Lt. Col. (Brevet Brigadier General) George Armstrong Custer found out the hard way. At the Battle of Little Big Horn in 1876, he failed to understand the size and resolve of the Native American forces he faced. He foolishly divided his forces, didn't make provisions for adequate ammunition and launched uncoordinated, mutually unsupporting attacks against a numerically superior and equally armed force. We all know what happened because Custer acted without first understanding the situation.

You cannot lead a successful organization without the right intel

As military service members, we understand that intel is a key success component of any military campaign. We must have an adequate understanding of key facts—about our own unit, the enemy's location, their strengths and movement. We must grasp what is going on around us in order to reach our objective and complete our mission.

The same principle applies in business. If you are going to lead a company to the place you envision, you MUST have the right intel. Let's make sure that we are clear on this: you cannot lead a successful organization without proper intel!

In **Vision (Chapter 1),** we shared how vision is vital to the success of your business. But, without good intel, you won't even know if it's possible to achieve your vision! Some of the important questions to keep in mind as you read this chapter include:

★ What are the key intel points I need to make my decisions?

★ What resource(s) do I need to obtain that intel and then analyze it effectively?

★ What kind of system do I need to regularly check/validate that the intel I am using is still valid and relevant to where I am in business?

The first thing that you must understand about gathering intel is that we're not talking about black ops, or CIA-type skullduggery. In the business context, intel means gathering information about the market, your organization and your competitors. It's not secretive, sexy, fun or exciting, which is exactly why many MVEs don't like to do it!

Let's face it. Most MVEs—including us—are action-oriented people. We want to get out and make things happen. Our energy now comes from getting things done out on the business battlefield. The whole idea of sitting down and doing research, connecting with the resources we need, or just finding out what those resources are, can be a challenge and major energy drain for us.

Another disconnect for many MVEs is that we find it easier to talk about vision than to gather information. Many of us are "big picture" people, and intel is, by its nature, detail-oriented. But the rewards for making the commitment to the sometimes tedious work of gathering intel, in effect doing what many of your potential competitors won't, are well worth it.

Sometimes MVEs miss the importance of things like intel and developing vision because, frankly, it's not talked about in the resources that most readily available to us. Often, MVEs who are either just starting a business, or wanting to take their business to another level, turn to classes or programs offered through the VA or the SBA.

We mentioned in this book's introduction that we believe the people who run these programs really do mean well. But our experience—

and the experience of scores of other MVEs we have interviewed—is that many MVEs come out of these classes/counseling programs more confused and less confident that they can succeed than before they started!

The keys to your success are not found in a slick business plan

Few of the successful MVEs we've talked to count the VA or SBA as resources they've used as a key part of their success. It ends up being more of a hindrance in many cases. Why? Because they focus on the wrong things: developing an exhaustive, old school, dust-collecting, 6-inch thick business plan, seeking traditional sources of financing that are very hard to come by (especially for innovative, but unproven, business ideas) and building a traditional, staff-heavy, bricks-and-mortar operation.

The keys to your success are not contained in a slick business plan. They will be found in the things we talk about in this book. (After all, unlike many of the teachers and counselors in the VA/SBA classes, we are actually *using* these principles to build and grow successful organizations.) We're not discounting the value of an action-oriented, user-oriented business plan. But there is a right way and a wrong way to write one. We want you to focus on vision, core values, mindset, and good intel—these are the real foundations for your long-term success!

Intel Insight

Throughout this chapter, we stress the value of developing relationships with more experienced people in your industry. It's one way to benefit from the wisdom of people who have been in the trenches long before you and have "been there, done that." So many otherwise smart business owners try to re-invent the wheel instead of truly understanding the value of learning from seasoned pros.

If you are new to a particular industry, a great way to gain hands-on experience is to get a job working for someone else in that industry for a year or two (or pursue an internship, especially if you have gone back to school). Spending some time on the frontlines in a new industry is far more valuable in most cases than theoretical case studies in a sterile academic environment.

Another excellent alternative is to partner with someone who has direct experience in the industry and who can act as a formal or informal advisor. This option is very similar to a junior officer leveraging the experience and wisdom of a senior NCO to drastically cut his or her learning curve and become a much more effective leader.

All of these are great ways to gain the knowledge and insight that you need in order to succeed in any industry, and to learn from the wisdom of others!

Since intel is so vital to your success, we will explore more fully how to gather it and what to do with the information once you get it. The good news? This is the best time ever to obtain solid intel on your target industry. Information that a decade ago cost thousands (or tens of thousands) of dollars to access through proprietary information gatekeepers is now readily available with a little bit of knowledge and a few mouse clicks.

It's never been easier (or cheaper) to get the information you need to explore whether your business idea is viable, what tools you need to develop and market your business, how you can build virtual teams to drastically lower on-going business costs, and how you can directly connect with your ideal client or customer. Unfortunately, this easy access to information is also a curse, since the sheer volume of information available and the need to sift through a lot of silt to uncover golden intel nuggets can be exhausting!

The ability to know whether your idea can be successful is really at the heart of gathering intel. If you find out that there is a place for your idea—that people want it, and you can carve out a spot for yourself in the market—it gives you the confidence to drive on. If you find out that your idea may not work in its current context, then you have the information you need to rethink your approach, or move on to another idea altogether.

No matter what you discover, intel is a critical first step in achieving success. So what are the best approaches to gathering the intel you need?

To lack intelligence is to be in the ring blindfolded.
—General David Shoup, USMC
(Former Commandant of the Marine Corps)

Intel is Like Homework— with the Key Being "Work"

At first glance, intel doesn't seem like it should be that hard… In its simplest form, intel includes 3 things:

★ Gathering information
★ Processing and analyzing that information
★ Disseminating and acting on that information

Of course, the first part—gathering—is easier to do if you are working in a field where you already have significant experience and contacts. In this case, connect with and leverage the resources you already know/have: your own experiences, current associates or colleagues, former colleagues, former bosses and managers and your industry contacts.

If you are starting out fresh in a new industry, it's more of a challenge. Where do you begin? Start by getting the big picture of your particular industry. This macro perspective will help you see the broad outline of your industry and gain answers to key questions, such as:

★ How large is the market?
★ What are the developing trends?
★ Who are the major players?
★ What are the opportunities and pitfalls?

Almost every industry has at least one trade or professional association and these are a great sources of initial information. These associations exist to provide people with facts and statistics about their industry, provide continuing education and connect the industry with their clients/customers and suppliers. Once you get the big picture and really understand the industry, you can start painting a detailed picture of your own business. Trade associations are a great place to start, but you will need more intel gathering in order to know whether your idea has what it takes.

The amount of data available today on any given industry is astounding. However, you must dig out and separate the relevant from the irrelevant and the actual "actionable intel" from the "nice to know" fluff.

Look for industry news reports, speeches given by key industry thought leaders, the presentation program or agenda for industry meetings or trade shows and anything else that provides a clear sight picture on what's hot. This may not be fun, exciting work, but the payoff can be huge!

In your research, you are likely to unearth a few nuggets of information that make all the difference to your business. You might discover an underserved niche or identify an emerging trend that you can step into on the ground floor. Often, existing players in the industry are too entrenched to even see the opportunity or aren't nimble enough to capitalize on a new trend, allowing fresh eyes and new ideas to make an immediate impact.

Anyone who has ever worked in a large, hide-bound organization knows that creating even the smallest change is akin to turning a battleship around in a bathtub...so opportunities to repackage or reposition current industry offerings or quickly take advantage of an industry-wide blind spot occur frequently!

Want to shorten your learning curve and gain a deeper perspective in a short amount of time? Seek out and connect with industry leaders: the people that are keynoting industry events, having articles written about them, receiving awards for innovation and challenging the status quo. Study them and find out what they are doing and how. Reach out and request an informational meeting to find out where they think the industry is headed.

You may be thinking "But why would somebody that important give me the time of day?"

If you approach them from a place of genuine curiosity and with a humble spirit, you will find that many top industry leaders are willing to answer questions. Many are passionate about creating change within their industry, and that change often comes from new blood. It's true, even with people you think are too busy to talk to you. But if you do get turned down, suck it up and move on to the next person.

★ ★ ★ ★ ★ ★ ★ ★ ★ ★ ★ ★ ★ ★ ★

Intel Insight

We cannot stress the importance of asking the experts in your industry enough. Some things are learned only after you immerse yourself in an area of study for a number of years.

The "10,000-Hour Rule" (based on the research of Dr. K. Anders Ericsson and popularized by author Malcolm Gladwell in his best-selling book *Outliers: The Story of Success*) holds that it takes a minimum of 10,000 hours of study and practice to achieve mastery in a subject or profession (about 20 hours a week for 10 years). You need to schedule time with people who have greater experience and wisdom, and ask them to share what they've learned.

You're probably wondering, "Aren't these people too busy to talk to me?" The answer is, in many cases, no!

Successful people often look for opportunities to give back and improve the industry that has been good to them. They will often give you an appointment so you can ask questions, if you follow a few simple rules:

★ Rule #1 - Be Specific
★ Rule #2 - Be Respectful of Their Time
★ Rule #3 - Be Thankful

Don't forget to thank them with a hand-written note or small thank you gift and look for ways to develop a long-term relationship, such as sending them a note when their company gets a big contract or is featured in a news story.

★ ★ ★ ★ ★ ★ ★ ★ ★ ★ ★ ★ ★ ★ ★ ★ ★

Most people love being in the role of a mentor or guru, and you should take advantage of that. Just remember to be respectful of that person's time and energy, and to give back as often as you can. You want to build mutually beneficial relationships with leaders in your industry. You can only do that if you are willing to give, as well as receive, help.

In the **Million Dollar Minute** exercise at the end of this chapter, we suggest several important areas of your industry on which to focus your intel gathering efforts. Even before that, we must stress one critically important intel area that, unfortunately, many smart, dedicated MVEs overlook; discovering whether your clients/customers actually *want* your product or service!

This may sound absurdly simple, but if nobody wants your product (or they don't see a need for it) they won't buy it. You would be shocked at the number of times we've had entrepreneurs tell us that they know exactly what customers need, and how they are going to educate customers to change their perception and make a fortune. Following this path without ever confirming that you are offering something people want is often a quick ticket to the poor house.

If nobody wants your product… *they won't buy it*

Maybe your idea *is* completely revolutionary and exactly what people need, but you'd better pay attention to what people want and incorporate that into your product or service. Otherwise, no one is going to give your product or service a chance, meaning they will never find out how great it is!

The problem? When you tell people that you have what they need, whether they want it or not, people often hear that as, "Hey! You are too dumb to know what's good for you. Let me tell you what you really need."

Nobody likes to be talked down to, so they'll immediately tune you out. Let's face it, if everyone did what they needed to do, we would all be skinny, rich and married to Mr. or Mrs. Right! Don't assume you know something (like what your customers want or need) without checking it out, and if you are trying to sell something that "fixes" people (or companies), it is imperative to carefully craft your marketing message to solve a "want."

For example, at the dawn of World War II, the French High Command was stuck in a mentality left over from World War I. They assumed the Germans "needed" to be faced with a defensive obstacle so daunting and formidable that all the horrors of the Great War would be magnified and they wouldn't dare attack. They likewise were convinced that what they needed was a solid, static defense that would delay the

Germans long enough to mobilize for a counter-offensive and therefore placed all of their trust in the impregnable Maginot Line.

Unfortunately, they let their "needs" get in the way of the German "wants", which was revenge for the humiliation of the Treaty of Versailles. The French also suffered some significant intel failures, such as assuming the Ardennes Forest was impassable to large bodies of mechanized troops. They treated it as a secure flank, trusting the Maginot Line would protect them from any German attack.

The Germans took advantage of French misconceptions and faulty intel. The main attack of their Blitzkrieg—or Lightening War—came right through the Ardennes, by-passed the Maginot Line, and raced across France to the English Channel in a week. The effect was so stunning that it forced the French to capitulate in a mere 6 weeks.

Good intel shows you where your product or service fits in the overall scheme of the market. It gives you the raw materials you need to build a battle plan for business success. Intel gathering is not easy or exciting, but it is absolutely necessary. But even the best intel is worthless if it isn't used properly. Next, we'll discuss how to analyze your intel and, more importantly, act on it.

> *In preparing for battle I have always found that*
> *plans are useless, but planning is indispensable.*
> —*General Dwight D. Eisenhower*

How to Analyze and Act Upon the Intel You Gather

Just gathering intel isn't enough. You must take the time to analyze and understand the intel. You must develop a course of action based on your analysis. Finally, you MUST take action!

One surefire recipe for business disaster is to attempt to analyze all the data yourself. There's an old proverb that states, "Plans go wrong for lack of advice; many advisers bring success."

As entrepreneurs, we sometimes develop blinders that only allow us to see things a certain way. We get too close to the situation and lack the perspective to put all the pieces together in a way that makes sense. Therefore, we all need a group of people that we can trust to give us their honest assessment, and provide an alternate viewpoint when we get too fixated on a particular course of action.

This is one of the values of developing relationships with people who have been in the trenches longer than ourselves. They often see things that we miss, either because we don't yet have the experience or because we are so focused on our "brilliant" idea that we don't see clearly or see the bigger picture.

The saying "none of us is as smart as all of us" is very true in business. So gather people you trust around you and enlist them to help you analyze and make sense of the intel with you. You will definitely discover more useful information than you would if you tried to do it all yourself.

★ ★ ★ ★ ★ ★ ★ ★ ★ ★ ★ ★ ★ ★ ★ ★ ★

Intel Insight

Go beyond just meeting with experts and try to establish a more formal mentoring relationship with an industry expert. As we shared in the previous Intel Insight, successful people enjoy sharing what they've learned. However, many people assume that they are unapproachable or—worse—only approach them from a position of "taking."

A more positive approach that carries a much higher success rate is to come from a place of service and either ask how you can be of service to them or how you can support them in getting their message out. Be prepared to give generously, as you may have a skill or experience that your mentor finds valuable.

The biggest key is to ask! Even if you think someone is too big or too busy to mentor you, you need to ask if such a relationship is possible. Too many entrepreneurs miss out on valuable opportunities because they fail to make the "big ask." Don't be one of them!

★ ★ ★ ★ ★ ★ ★ ★ ★ ★ ★ ★ ★ ★ ★ ★ ★

For many MVEs, gathering intel isn't the problem (although it is tedious work). Analyzing the data isn't even that difficult. The hardest part is taking action on what we learn. We are convinced that the ability to take action is one of the key success factors that separate exceptional entrepreneurs from mediocre ones, and we devote **Rapid Action (Chapter 6)** to developing this concept more fully.

In order for your intel to be useful, you must do something with it. You must get the relevant pieces of information to the people who need it, such as team members, investors and key advisors. Want to put your banker to sleep? Load up your business plan with all the facts you have discovered. Want to confuse your team members? Drop a ream of raw data on their desks without running it through your "vision" filter, and expect them to work miracles with it.

As the leader, visionary, and driver for your company, you are ultimately responsible for getting the right information into the right hands, providing strategic direction and then acting on what you discover.

Inaction is far worse than failure for an entrepreneur

During the first Gulf War, General Norman Schwarzkopf and his staff used the intel at his disposal to develop the "Big Left Hook." The plan? Flank and bypass the bulk of the entrenched Iraqi forces, roll up their flank, engage and destroy their "elite" Republican Guard divisions and cut their supply lines. The Iraqis were so thoroughly defeated that the war was effectively over in 96 hours. The Allies used their intel and analysis to take massive, decisive action!

Inaction is far worse than failure for an entrepreneur. Once you've taken action, you may realize you've taken a wrong turn. What should you do? Move on! Take course corrective action along the way. Chances are, you're now smarter and wiser than before you started, so just endeavor not to make the same mistake twice. Further, don't beat yourself up over the mistakes you make—and you will make them! Finally, whatever you do, don't listen to the naysayers who ask "Why don't you just get a real job?" or otherwise try to tear you down.

All entrepreneurs want their businesses to get off the ground smoothly. For some, the first time they hit resistance, or when they realize they are heading down the wrong road, they become paralyzed. Sometimes the paralysis results in the inability to take another decisive action step after making a big mistake. Other times, fear comes as a result of running into some resistance; maybe from friends, family, industry experts or even competitors. They recoil from the pushback and sit there with their engine idling, going nowhere. Don't let this happen to you!

Every entrepreneur will have failures (trust us, we know from intimate, first-hand experience). Ben Franklin put it this way: "Success is moving from failure to failure without losing your enthusiasm." It is crucial that you understand this concept.

Soichiro Honda, the Japanese industrialist and founder of Honda Motor said that success is 99 percent failure. The reality is every entrepreneur is going to make mistakes.

However, the way you recover from a mistake or setback often makes all the difference between ultimate failure and success. Our advice? When you realize you've made a mistake, re-assess immediately, check your map and get back to the right road. You cannot let fear, embarrassment or anything else keep you from taking immediate course corrective action and forging ahead.

A critical corollary to our admonition above is: don't fall so in love with your own brilliant idea that you refuse to adjust your course or change tactics when necessary!

We often find this occurs when you attempt to sell people what you think they need as opposed to what they want, as we discussed earlier in this chapter. Just to reinforce, you can avoid this by building a trusted team of advisors, mentors and mastermind partners to assist you in analyzing, organizing and vetting data before you act on it.

Remember, when you become too enamored with your own ideas, you tend to become very stubborn and turn into a French general!

Prepare for the unknown by studying how others in the past have coped with the unforeseeable and the unpredictable.
—General George S. Patton, Jr.

Million Dollar Minute

Part 1:

Now it's time to test your current intel on your business and industry. Spend 2 minutes in each category, writing down everything you know about the following:

★ Your own product/service/business.
★ Your competition.
★ Current economic opportunities and challenges in general, and for your product/service/business in particular.
★ Any other key items for which you still need answers.

How is your intel? Do you feel good about what you know? Where are the gaps in your intel, and how can you fill those gaps?

Part 2:

Take 5 minutes, and write down the name of every expert in your industry you would like to spend an hour with. Write down a few reasons why you want to meet with that particular person.

After you've made your list, develop and execute a plan to connect with them.

COACHING

★ ★ ★ ★ ★ ★ ★ ★ ★ ★ ★ ★ ★ ★ ★ ★ ★ ★ ★

The notice of others has been the start of many successful men.
—General George Patton, Jr.

Key Challenge

Most entrepreneurs, including MVEs, are too close to their own situation to make critical decisions with any level of objectivity. In addition, they sometimes lack the experience, network and resources that make all the difference between creating enduring success and suffering eternal mediocrity.

All Top Achievers Have Coaches to Help Them Reach the Next Level

Too many MVEs buy into the myth and romance, perpetuated by popular media, of the Lone Wolf entrepreneur. Buying into this "go it alone" fable on your entrepreneurial journey is very dangerous to both your short and long-term success. Falling prey to the Lone Wolf storyline also virtually guarantees you will struggle harder, waste more time and money and take longer to achieve that success (if you make it at all).

Are there occasional Lone Wolf success stories? Sure. However, objective analysis of their arduous path to eventual success often reflects decisions made from stubbornness and pride rather than clear strategic vision, determination and true grit.

Every world-class athlete, entertainer, and entrepreneur has coaches

The truth? Every world-class athlete, entertainer and entrepreneur has coaches and mentors. Pause for a moment and reflect on this…how many true top performers are you aware of that reached the pinnacle of success as a Lone Wolf?

★ ★ ★ ★ ★ ★ ★ ★ ★ ★ ★ ★ ★ ★ ★ ★ ★

Intel Insight

The Myth of the Lone Wolf Entrepreneur

We believe that the Lone Wolf entrepreneur is one of the most destructive myths that MVEs run into on a constant basis. This myth is a staple in popular media: TV shows, movies, and even some business magazines and business-related TV shows perpetuate this idea that most entrepreneurs become successful on their own. They pull themselves up by their bootstraps— they didn't need any help to succeed.

We won't say there are no Lone Wolf success stories out there. But, if you look behind the curtain of those stories, you'll find they had team members, coaches, mentors and advisors that empowered them to beat the odds.

> Lone Wolves make for great stories of rugged individualism, but the truth is, if you really want to achieve sustained success, you need coaches and mentors to guide you along the way!

This has certainly been our personal experience in both the military and in business. In fact, the vast majority of our biggest business failures and frustrations occurred when we tried to go it alone. Conversely, many of our biggest successes map directly to receiving counsel and guidance from smarter and wiser coaches, mentors and advisors that are farther along the entrepreneurial path. Having learned the hard way, we will personally never operate our current or future businesses without engaging top business coaches and participating in peer-to-peer masterminds.

The bottom line? This entrepreneurial gig is tough enough without hamstringing yourself by falling for the Lone Wolf myth and trying to figure all this out on your own!

These critical success multipliers go by different names, such as coach, mentor, teacher or advisor. You might develop a formal mentor/mentee relationship or your coach may just be someone you call when you need a fresh set of eyes on a problem. The actual title and form of the relationship isn't really that important. The point is that you need a trusted advisor, someone farther down the road than you are, to help you reach the highest levels of success in the shortest time possible.

MVEs sometimes have trouble asking for help because we are a self-reliant bunch. We believe we should be able to figure everything out on our own and make it all work without anyone's help. We pick up this attitude because we can take care of many things on our own.

Unfortunately, sometimes this translates into us thinking, "Don't ask for help. It's a sign of weakness." Which, of course, couldn't be further from the truth.

The truth is, we have coaches and mentors throughout our military careers. We called them by different names, such as instructor, team leader, platoon leader or company commander; but these folks were coaches and mentors.

★ ★ ★ ★ ★ ★ ★ ★ ★ ★ ★ ★ ★ ★ ★ ★ ★ ★

Intel Insight

Mentors Make A Huge Difference
Phil Dyer, CFP®, RLP®, CPCC
America's Entrepreneur Strategist

When I arrived in Germany as a wet-behind-the-ears Second Lieutenant fresh out of the Armor Officer Basic Course at Ft. Knox, Kentucky, I possessed tons of theoretical book knowledge, but I didn't really know how to apply that knowledge to real-world situations.

Fortunately, I was smart enough to recognize what I didn't know. I valued my platoon sergeant's practical experience and engaged him as my mentor. While it was my platoon and I took leadership responsibility, I routinely sought his advice in key areas of professional development. We created a very good working relationship which got my military career off to a great start. What do you think would have happened if I had employed the Lone Wolf approach and discounted his years of experience, or if he had been uninterested in being a true mentor?

This is why coaches and mentors are so important. They can clearly see where you have gaps in your knowledge or experience and fill in those holes. They can help you apply the knowledge you do possess in different ways to achieve desired results faster. Finally, they can help you connect the dots and see the bigger picture.

Seeing the big picture clearly is often very difficult for entrepreneurs. We are so close to our businesses: heads down and working frantically to make deadlines, get proposals, completed projects or finished products out the door, that we can't accurately or objectively judge what's transpiring. We may miss opportunities that are literally right in front of us, overlook a critical systems flaw that can completely derail us, or simply be operating on four cylinders instead of eight. The right coach or mentor can help us step back, take in the bigger picture and give us the perspective that we must have for sustained success.

In our experience, there are a number of ways in which the right coach helps you achieve a high level of enduring success, including:

★ **The external view:** The coach brings perspective you don't possess because you are too close to your business or too far down in the weeds. This external view is critical when making strategic decisions. The coach helps you see what must be done, because he/she doesn't have the emotional investment in your business that you do.

★ **Challenging preconceived notions:** Because coaches have a different set of knowledge and experience, they challenge you on things you just assume to be true. Too often, decisions on what actions to take are based on a view of reality that may not be accurate. The coaches help you see past these self-imposed blinders.

★ **Evaluating failures:** As we shared in the last chapter, every entrepreneur will have failures and the most important thing is to learn from those failures. Conducting an effective after-action review is critical; otherwise you won't internalize the lesson and make timely adjustments. The coach provides the framework and support for meaningful review and keeps you focused on taking course corrective action and moving forward instead of beating yourself up or wallowing in self-pity.

★ **Truth-telling:** It's really easy to fall in love with our own brilliant idea and surround ourselves with people who will tell us what we want to hear, instead of what we need to hear. This is especially true as your organization grows and these people are on your payroll! The coach is sufficiently removed from your circle and has your permission to tell you the unvarnished truth, even when you might not want to hear it.

★ **Cheerleading:** The coach is there to celebrate your successes. It's always great to get a pat on the back, especially from someone else who also enjoys a significant level of success. More importantly, the coach helps you objectively evaluate your "secret success sauce" so you can see how you achieved it and learn to repeat it!

Entrepreneurship can be a lonely endeavor, especially since well-meaning spouses, family and friends who simply don't get the entrepreneurial mindset, can easily tear you down without even realizing it. The simple fact that the coach is a kindred spirit who intimately understands the entrepreneurial journey is hugely important when you hit the inevitable rough patch.

Many MVEs intellectually understand that a coach is just as

necessary in business as trainers, mentors and advisors were during their time in the military. Unfortunately, many stop there and don't take making the connection with the right coach or mentor past an intellectual exercise. All too often, they get stuck in the "How":

★ How will I know when it is time to hire a coach?
★ How will I know where to find the right coach?
★ How will I know if I am getting my money's worth?
★ How will I know when it is time to move on from a coaching relationship?

We will answer these questions (and more) in the next section and provide concrete examples of the power of coaching!

> *I absolutely believe that people, unless coached,*
> *never reach their maximum capabilities.*
> —*Bob Nardelli, former CEO of Home Depot*

Finding The Right Coach For You

There is no doubt that a great coach/mentor can help you reach the highest levels of success in virtually all areas of business and life. But how do you find the coach that's right for you? First, seek out a coach specializing in the area you desire to see specific growth. While we are focused on business growth in this book, coaches and mentors are also critical in fueling personal, spiritual, relational and professional growth. We personally use coaches to guide us in each of these areas when we are feeling stuck, restless or lost.

You might be thinking "OK, enough already! I get that I need a coach, but where do I go to find one?" This is often a major challenge, since there are tens of thousands of people out there who market themselves as business and/or life coaches (a Google search for "business coach" returns about 14 million results and the term "life coach" returns a staggering 95 million hits). There is virtually no entry barrier to becoming a coach and many will gladly coach you for $100 or $200 per month. Unfortunately, many self-styled "business experts" out there are barely scraping by and may be looking at you as their next car payment. Sure, they're cheap, but this is absolutely an area that you get exactly what you pay for.

The right coach is like a super-strength bottle of Windex

There's an old maxim that says: "You can't lead someone where you've never been." This is a major potential pitfall when engaging a coach. You may find someone who talks a good game, has a slick website or who promises amazing riches and success if you become a client or buy their system. They look perfect, but when you pull back the curtain and look a bit more carefully, they don't have the track record to match the hype!

The right coach is like a super-strength bottle of Windex. Sometimes, being in business feels like you're trying to drive down a narrow highway at 90 miles per hour with fogged-up, dirty windows and a 1,000-foot drop off either side of the road. One false move and you are headed for disaster! A good coach will help you wipe away the grime and gain crystal clarity. They help you zero in on specific targets, internalize lessons from your successes and failures and help you map out the most direct route to your objective.

You want someone who will challenge you to step up, break

through the visible and invisible barriers keeping you stuck and push through powerfully to the next level! Top business coaches and mentors have vast reservoirs of experience, information and connections. They carry toolboxes filled with a variety of strategies to support you in making the leap from where you are to where you want to be. These coaches have expansive networks and will leverage those networks to connect you with other key experts, possible clients/customers and strategic partners. This type of coach is incredibly valuable and should be viewed as an investment, not an expense.

Intel Insight

Finding the right coach

How do you find a coach to help you get to the next level? Word of mouth, specific knowledge of your industry/clients/customers and a proven record of success are all key markers to seek. Chances are you know someone right now who is currently engaging a coach (or has in the recent past). Look for recommendations from people you know and trust.

Once you obtain some recommendations, gather some intel on each coach. Check out testimonials from past clients; ask about their coaching philosophy, their metrics for success and the tools they use. Do a "gut check" to see if the coach seems like a good fit. In most cases, you want someone who has "been there and done that," someone who has walked the path that you are on and is at least a bit farther ahead on his/her entrepreneurial journey. While the coach doesn't necessarily need to be an expert in your specific industry, they should have proven success in working with business owners just like you.

As discussed in **Intel (Chapter 2)**, don't discount creating a more informal mentorship relationship with someone you respect that meets the criteria for a good coach. Just remember to approach them with an attitude of service so you are offering something of value while you are learning from them.

★ ★ ★ ★ ★ ★ ★ ★ ★ ★ ★ ★ ★ ★ ★ ★ ★

A good coach can easily return 5, 10 or even 20-fold your investment in them

Engaging top business coaches takes commitment and the willingness to invest in your most valuable business asset...you! Rates vary broadly; depending on the type of engagement, method of coaching delivery, how much direct access you have to the coach (as opposed to their team) and what you are trying to accomplish in the coaching relationship. Typical investment levels include:

★ $50-$100 per month for informational programs with little direct access to the top coach
★ $500-$2,000 per month for more direct hands-on coaching with regular calls
★ $10,000 a day (or more) for a 1-on-1 VIP day with the coach

Okay, you may be thinking, "There is no way in hell I would pay that much for a coach!" We get it. We have been there before and thought exactly the same thing. Let us pose this question, "How expensive is it to be stuck in neutral, not being able to grow your business, connect with the right clients and hire the right staff?" A good coach can easily return 5, 10 or even 20-fold your investment in them. We have both experienced explosive growth in multiple businesses after engaging the right coach.

We close out this section with several final thoughts on coaches and coaching relationships:

★ **You will have a number of coaches as you advance through your Vetrepreneur career.** Smart business owners engage coaches to help them achieve the next level of success or overcome a specific challenge or obstacle that is keeping them stuck. Once you have grown past the point where that coach can assist you; it may be time to move on to another. Chances are, you will make a mistake and hire the wrong coach one day. As we stated earlier, failure is part of being an entrepreneur. So don't let hiring a bad coach sour you on coaching. Learn from the experience and drive on! We've made major mistakes investing in coaches and coaching programs…it happens! However, the lessons that we ultimately learned from those mistakes are priceless!

★ **Caution! Never work with a coach who himself is not an active participant in a coaching or mentoring program.** The moment someone thinks they "know it all," is the exact moment in time you want to get far away from them. We won't work with coaches or mentors who are not continually learning and expanding their own knowledge base and network.

Ready to learn about the top entrepreneurs' "Secret Weapon?" We divulge an incredibly powerful business and wealth multiplier in the next section.

Advice after the mischief is like medicine after death.
—*Danish proverb*

Mastermind Groups are Solid "Success Foundations" for Most Top Entrepreneurs

For some reading this book, the term "Mastermind Group" may be new. Or, maybe you've heard the phrase, but you're unclear about the meaning. Basically, a Mastermind Group is a group of peers that come together on a regular schedule (annually, quarterly, monthly, or weekly) to mutually support each other's businesses, solve tough entrepreneur challenges, share marketing and business growth ideas and even connect fellow members with business opportunities.

Every mastermind group is different. Some are very informal roundtables, a group of peers that rotate the leadership position within the group, and everyone takes turns talking. Other mastermind groups are much more formal, with established leadership and rules. Some meet only by phone, others only in person, although most use a combination of the two.

We've personally witnessed the creation of multi-million dollar ideas in mastermind groups

Smart entrepreneurs invest heavily to participate in the right mastermind group. Most good masterminds require a financial commitment of $7,500 to $15,000 annually and top entrepreneurs routinely invest $250,000 (or more) to participate in very high-level groups. Before you throw down this book in disgust and call these folks a bunch of fools, try to get your brain around the lifetime value of a single major business breakthrough or great idea. We've personally witnessed the creation of multi-million dollar ideas in mastermind groups. It's actually quite common and very exciting!

Most top groups are very structured and participants are serious about their own business and about helping others succeed. You get the opportunity to present your biggest business challenge or idea before the group. After the presentation, other group members ask clarifying questions and then you move on to a group brainstorming session. These sessions can be very unpredictable!

Members often come up with completely new ways for you to get something done, vastly improve on your idea or even tell you the idea isn't worth pursuing. The room is often filled with electric energy as members problem-solve and explore possibilities from a dozen different angles. The power of having 8-12 brilliant entrepreneurial minds focused on your business idea or challenge is incredible, and this is the true genius of the Mastermind format.

★ ★ ★ ★ ★ ★ ★ ★ ★ ★ ★ ★ ★ ★ ★ ★

Intel Insight

Anatomy of a Successful Mastermind Group

We find that great mastermind groups have four things in common:

★ **Financial commitment.** Most good mastermind groups require that members pay to become part of the group. This ensures that each participant is really committed to giving his or her full attention to the time the group spends together.

★ **Structure.** The group must have a pre-defined plan for

meetings, including someone to facilitate the discussions. Otherwise, the meetings can devolve into chaos, with very little being accomplished.

★ **Confidentiality.** Each member of the group must sign and adhere to a written confidentiality agreement. This is non-negotiable. Group discussions need to stay within the group.

★ **Accountability.** Group members need to be accountable for several things, among them preparing to speak at each meeting, and being ready to give advice and counsel to other members. Each group member should also be expected to take action on the issues they discuss with the group. Group meetings aren't gripe-fests; group members participate to gain clarity so they can take steps forward.

Steer clear of groups that cut corners in any of these areas.

★ ★ ★ ★ ★ ★ ★ ★ ★ ★ ★ ★ ★ ★ ★ ★

One of the reasons that mastermind groups can be so effective is that people pay good money to be part of the group. That means two things. First, it means people come prepared. They are ready to discuss the problems that keep their businesses from moving forward. Before the group comes together, everyone has thought through what they are going to say, they've done their homework. That makes the time productive for everyone.

Second, the fact that people pay to be part of the group means that they come ready to help other people. There is an expectation that everyone in the group will help each other. People give their attention to what others are saying. There's a real spirit of cooperation, and a desire that everyone in the group succeeds. That means you get the best from everyone there.

One aspect of mastermind groups that make them so dynamic is that they consist of people from different backgrounds, with different areas of expertise. One member may own a public relations business, while another runs a security business, another is a CPA, and yet another is a martial arts instructor. With that much variety in the room, you know that problems will be examined from many different angles.

An effective mastermind group also holds you accountable to take action on the things that are preventing you from moving forward. Once you've brought up a problem for the group to discuss, you can't come back to the next meeting without having taken action. It's a great source of motivation for those who tend to put off facing problems.

There are two main concerns that sometimes keep people away from mastermind groups, but they really shouldn't. The first concern is about confidentiality. After all, you're sharing problems and ideas with a room full of people. Couldn't one of them steal your idea for a product or service, implement it, and make money from your idea?

In reality, this doesn't happen. First of all, good mastermind groups consist of people who are there to serve and give, not to steal. To ensure that no one steals intellectual property, everyone involved must sign a confidentiality agreement. This ensures that the issues discussed within the group stay there.

The second concern that many people have is about people soliciting their services within the group. After all, if you have a PR guy and a copywriter in your group, what keeps them from using the mastermind meeting to drum up new business for themselves?

In a good mastermind group, this rarely happens. People are there to give and receive feedback, not to self-promote. Mastermind meetings are not networking events, where you hand out business cards and try to sign up new clients. Most groups that we know police themselves, if someone is there to promote their business, other members of the group can ask them to stop or leave.

We find that we often leave mastermind group meetings with page after page of great ideas. We learn from people talking about our own problems. We also learn from participating in group discussions about the problems that other people face. Mastermind groups are a combination of advisory panel, support group, accountability partners, and cheerleading section.

★ ★ ★ ★ ★ ★ ★ ★ ★ ★ ★ ★ ★ ★ ★ ★ ★ ★

Intel Insight

It's Lonely at the Top

We've spoken with many people who are leaders of large organizations. One thing that seems to be true for many of them is that being at the top of a company can be extremely lonely. It is not practical for them to go to their subordinates to kick around some of their more potent ideas. They may not have a management team that they can depend on to explore different business options. So, they are left to make decisions on their own.

This is where a coach or mastermind group can be very helpful. A leader can get honest feedback, share business ideas in a safe environment and even get their butt kicked if necessary. A coaching/mastermind arrangement can provide a safe place for leaders to give and get good business advice, without worrying about what people will do with the information.

★ ★ ★ ★ ★ ★ ★ ★ ★ ★ ★ ★ ★ ★ ★ ★ ★ ★

It's not a coincidence that most of the successful entrepreneurs we know are part of mastermind groups. They will stretch you, make you think about things in different ways, and force you to deal with the problems that you face. Take advantage of this "secret weapon" of successful entrepreneurs!

> *To act in concert with a great man is the first of blessings.*
> —*Marquis de Lafayette, 1778, letter to General George Washington*

Million Dollar Minute

Part 1:

Think about a military or business experience where you connected with the right coach or mentor. What challenge did that connection help you to solve? What was the value to you personally and professionally?

Now connect with the present day. What major obstacle or challenge are you currently facing in your business? Is a portion of your business start-up plan driving you crazy? What other area of your life would improve if you connected with someone who could help you work through it from a place of experience and knowledge?

By this time next week, find a coach to help you tackle your biggest frustration!

Part 2:

Do a self-assessment of your skills, resources, talents and experiences. What could you add to a mastermind group that would be valuable to the other members? Remember, the success of the group depends on its members showing up ready to give generously.

Also don't discount a skill or talent just because you can do it easily. Focusing on that which comes effortlessly to you, but is very difficult or virtually impossible for others to master is a great way to quickly grow your business and provide lasting value.

TEAM

★ ★ ★ ★ ★ ★ ★ ★ ★ ★ ★ ★ ★ ★ ★ ★ ★ ★

Individuals play the game, but teams beat the odds.
—Special Ops maxim

Key Challenge

Too many MVEs buy into the Lone Wolf myth of successful entrepreneurship. They try to do too many things themselves and never build an effective team. No organization will create enduring success without a highly effective team.

Every Successful MVE Needs a Great Team

Based on **Coaching (Chapter 3)**, we trust you recognize the Lone Wolf approach to Vetrepreneur® success is a bad idea! It significantly limits your ability to effectively start and grow your business on virtually every front. Fully understanding this doesn't apply to just coaching and mentoring, it is also crucial when building a winning team. We'll be blunt; you will never create the business you envision, the life you desire or create the positive impact you are capable of without the right team in place.

When we first mention "building a team," many aspiring

Vetrepreneurs® break into a cold sweat as visions of payroll taxes, micromanagement headaches and "herding cats" flash before them. The truth? Teams come in many forms, from 100 percent virtual teams that you pay as independent contractors to the traditional multi-location organization structure with hundreds, thousands or tens of thousands of team members. The principles of team building we share in this chapter are universal, no matter what the size or complexity of the business.

★ ★ ★ ★ ★ ★ ★ ★ ★ ★ ★ ★ ★ ★ ★ ★ ★

Intel Insight

The Lone Wolf Approach = Burnout
Phil Dyer, CFP®, RLP®, CPCC
America's Entrepreneur Strategist

I proudly adopted the Lone Wolf mentality for several years when I first got started in business and it almost killed me! I thought it was faster and easier to simply do everything myself and I didn't want to mess with the management and paperwork hassles of traditional employees. If I wanted to increase my income, I just got a few more clients and worked that much harder.

Before long, my weekly work commitment surged into the 70+ hour range and I was juggling way too many balls in the air. After several years at this pace, I hit what I refer to as the "time-money wall." It took a health scare, which fortunately turned out to be nothing, along with an in-depth conversation with one of my mentors to gain a new perspective. I began to strategically outsource essential tasks that I either didn't enjoy, wasn't very good at, or didn't interest me. The more I outsourced, delegated and deleted, the more time I created to focus on the core of my business and spend time with my wife and children.

I am somewhat employee-phobic; I choose to support my multiple businesses with a virtual team. It works so well that I recently took a 2 week trip to the Italian countryside and completely unplugged…no computer, no phone, no Blackberry, no business books or magazines for the entire time. My business didn't even miss me, and my family had my undivided attention!

★ ★ ★ ★ ★ ★ ★ ★ ★ ★ ★ ★ ★ ★ ★ ★

In fact, huge leaps in technology and connectivity make crafting a team of extraordinary talent from all around the world exceptionally easy. You can hire to specific tasks from people that do amazing work for a fraction of the cost of a traditional full-time employee. This is tremendously beneficial for those MVEs in start-up mode, when capital is usually very tight!

Also note that we used the term "team member" instead of "employee." We firmly believe that team member is far more positive than employee and better reflects rapidly changing business dynamics. Being a team member is all about shared vision and empowerment as opposed to servant vs. overseer relationships.

Be cautious about fixating on preconceived ideas about what your team should look like, especially ideas that originate from conventional wisdom. The important initial step is building a team to support your mission-critical tasks now and for the next 1-2 years. Don't lock yourself into a long-term team structure, since your needs will likely change significantly as your business grows, the marketplace shifts and new technologies develop. Focus on your vision for future success, but allow for substantial flexibility as you look ahead 5 to 15 years and beyond.

The most important element in building a good team is knowing yourself

Without question, the most important, and, unfortunately, most frequently overlooked, element in building a good team is you knowing yourself well. We will explore this further later, but try to avoid the common mistake of hiring people who are just like you. Hire people who complement you, cover gaps in your knowledge or experience, provide foundational support for your weaknesses and allow you to fully focus on your strengths.

The *StrengthsFinder 2.0* and the *Kolbe A Index* assessments we recommend are great tools to more fully connect you with your inherent strengths and passions. They give you an objective picture of how you should be spending your time, and how best to approach tasks.

Let's face it…it's hard for many of us to admit that we aren't great at everything. We are often taught to spend inordinate amounts of time trying to "fix" our perceived weaknesses instead of focusing on our extraordinary strengths. The truth is that you are not good at everything. Heck, you might not be good at most things!

That said, we believe that you possess a unique combination of 3-5 core abilities where you are simply brilliant. These are your strengths, the areas you should focus on with laser-like intensity while outsourcing, delegating or deleting everything else to your custom-built team.

STOP! If you haven't done so yet, please stop reading right now and take the *StrengthsFinder 2.0* and *Kolbe A Index* assessments (you can find the links in the back of the book or on our companion website at **www.VictorySuccessResources.com**). The insights you gain are invaluable guides as you begin to build your team.

On a related note, this is a good time to review the material in **Vision (Chapter 1)**. We'll explain to you the importance of hiring people who buy into your vision. Be sure your vision is clear in your own mind; if you don't have clarity about your vision, neither will the people you hire!

We find there are three common misconceptions that prevent MVEs from starting or expanding their team, even when they KNOW they need to do so. They are:

★ **It takes too long to train someone:** It's true that training team members takes time. But if you clearly identify your vision and values and hire people who buy into your vision, your training will result in a team member that magnifies the strength and effectiveness of your organization.

★ **It's quicker and easier to do things yourself:** When you first hire someone, you probably can do their job more quickly than they can. You can also probably do it better than they can. The question is, are you doing the things at which you excel, the things that will result in long-term success for your business, or are you busy doing the things that others should be doing? Your team members will increase their speed and efficiency as they gain experience, provided you hire the right people.

★ **It's too expensive to hire a team:** When you try to do everything yourself, you waste time and energy doing things that don't build your business, thereby significantly limiting your success. Your team expands your ability to do what you're best at, freeing you up to succeed. It's better to look at it this way: it's too expensive not to hire a team!

The last misconception gets to the heart of the problem. Too many entrepreneurs see hiring team members, coaches, or anything else that doesn't physically put dollars into their bank account, as expenses. In reality, they are investments in the future success of your business. When you have the right people around you, your opportunities to build long-term success expand exponentially. The money you spend in training and developing your team members will result in a stronger, more effective organization.

You may be thinking, "This all sounds well and good, but how the heck do I do this when I am already time and cash-starved?" We dive deep into this in the next section.

Individual commitment to a group effort—that is what makes a team work, a company work, a society work, a civilization work.
—Vince Lombardi, NFL Coach and Assistant Coach at West Point

How to Build a Team that Ensures Long-Term Success

It takes much more than warm bodies to make a team. A team is a group of people who subscribe to a common mission. They are willing to work with and support each other for a greater good. This is the reason that your biggest task in team building is to effectively communicate your vision and values to the team.

You must communicate the vision and values of your company early on in the hiring process. You need to be clear, open and honest about what's important in your organization. When you state your values and vision from the very beginning of the hiring process, it is much easier to attract the right people and weed out the wrong people. People who buy into your vision will be much more motivated to accomplish great things for your organization.

A man does not get killed for a half-pence a day or petty distinctions.
You must speak to the soul in order to electrify him.
—*Napoleon Bonaparte*

We believe it is imperative to focus your team building efforts on those with shared vision, values and several other key traits. We also believe far too many entrepreneurs overemphasize the importance of skills and experience when hiring. People can learn new skills and can gain experience, but it is very difficult to "train" certain traits into someone...they either have it or they don't!

There are three traits that can't be taught, and that you shouldn't waste time trying to teach, that all of your potential team members must possess. These traits are motivation, integrity and the capacity to grow.

Your team members must be motivated, they need to "bring it" each day and on every project. However, motivation without integrity is dangerous. You'll end up with someone who wants to get things done and achieve, but they are willing to cut corners and act against your core values to accomplish their goals. Finally, if you hire people who possess both motivation and integrity, but lack the capacity to grow, they will eventually slow down, or even stop, the forward progress of your organization.

Intel Insight

Motivation, Integrity and the Capacity to Grow

Too many MVEs hire team members based solely on the new hire's experience, knowledge or skill set. We believe this can be a mistake. You can teach people knowledge and skills. You cannot teach integrity and core values. Thus, integrity and core values are the first things to look for when you hire someone.

A new team member who buys into your corporate vision and possesses integrity will be an asset to your company, even if you need to fill in gaps in their knowledge or skill set. Look for those innate qualities in every person you hire.

Ideally, you want someone to possess all three character traits, share your values, and who has the experience and skills you need. But if you find someone who's motivated, has integrity, can grow with your company and who shares your values, hire them immediately, even if they don't have all the experience you want. Experience can be taught; critical traits and core values cannot.

One reason it's so important to hire people with these traits is that it only takes one bad team member to disrupt and poison an effective team. A person who lacks integrity will cost you customers and ultimately your reputation. An unmotivated team member is an anchor that will hold your organization down and adversely affect the morale of others.

Slow to Hire, Quick to Fire

It's difficult to fire a team member, especially if that person is successful or possesses a skill that is difficul to acquire. Therefore, many business owners, especially in the early stages, will turn a blind eye to the shortcomings of someone who is bringing revenue into their companies. Our experience is that it's better to fire people quickly, before they have the chance to wreck the morale and effectiveness of the rest of the team. Our mantra is "slow to hire, quick to fire."

That's not to say you should fire people for silly reasons, but when you see that someone is not working out, it's best to sever the relationship as soon as possible. If you have current team members, most of them probably work on an at-will basis, meaning that you can let them go at any time. Of course, make sure you document all of your conversations and all of the different ways you tried to get their performance up to speed. But when someone is a poor fit for your company in the beginning, they will still be a poor fit 1, 5 or 10 years down the line. We know it can be challenging, but it's best to fire them quickly.

Ensure that you protect yourself by having a written set of standard procedures in place that fully outlines your process for hiring, working with and, when needed, firing team members who aren't working out. We'll share more about creating effective standard operating procedures in **OPS (Chapter 5)**.

We strongly recommend all new hires for your team go through a 90-day probationary period, during which you can let them go for virtually any reason. This three-month "test drive" will allow you to answer some key questions:

★ Does the new hire really understand your vision and values?
★ Are they self-motivated?
★ Do they have the integrity you demand from team members?
★ Are they are a quick learner who will continuously grow with your company?

Chances are you will know all these answers within the first two weeks of the introductory period. It's much like dating someone. You can usually tell after 1 or 2 dates whether you and the other person are compatible. We hate hearing stories of Vetrepreneurs® holding on until day 88 or 89 of the introductory period in the forlorn hope that the poor fit hire will miraculously turn around.

If the new hire isn't working out, be open and honest about it and then let them go as early as possible. Otherwise, you waste your valuable time and energy along with theirs. Don't let the right person for your team slip away because you're too busy trying to fix someone who is a bad fit.

We will cover how to figure out exactly who you want on your team, and how you forge those people into an effective "kick-ass" team in the next section.

An Army is a team, lives, sleeps, fights, and eats as a team.
This individual hero stuff is a bunch of crap.
—General George S. Patton, Jr

Building Your Team for Peak Performance (and Keeping it There)

Many entrepreneurs share a common weakness: We tend to hire people just like us! We call this the "Mini-Me" syndrome (with apologies to Mike Meyers). We've fallen into this trap when building both traditional and virtual teams and it's certainly understandable.

There is comfort and familiarity when hiring people with a similar background to our own. Parallel skills sets, shared experiences and similar world views feed this comfort level. You tend to look at things the same way, use the same problem solving approaches and even come to the exact same solutions. Sounds great, right? Our answer is an emphatic "NO!" This is usually a terrible way to build an effective team.

If you succumb to the Mini-Me syndrome, your team will let many critical functions fall through the cracks. Why? If your team has all of the same strengths, it stands to reason they also share the same weaknesses and blind spots. Everyone will avoid the weak spots and these important tasks will pile up until they become overwhelming!

Instead, hire strategically. Hire people who complement your strengths and interests; find people that excel doing tasks that are not your strength, but that they love doing. They will pick up the slack in the areas where you are the weakest. This is why self-knowledge of inherent strengths and passions is essential and why we stress the assessments we mentioned in the Introduction and first section of this chapter. Without this knowledge, it's hard to even know where to begin building your team. Once you obtain this knowledge, you can act to quickly fill the gaps.

★ ★ ★ ★ ★ ★ ★ ★ ★ ★ ★ ★ ★ ★ ★ ★

Intel Insight

Just Because I Can...

Just because you CAN do something doesn't mean you SHOULD do it. The "Pareto Principle" states that 80 percent of your results in business, and in life, come from just 20 percent of your activity. For example, most companies find that around 80 percent of their revenues come from 20 percent of their customers, and 20 percent of their sales staff make about 80 percent of the company's sales.

How does this apply to you? You must concentrate your efforts on the fewest activities that deliver the most benefit. Most MVEs do far too many things in their organizations, spread themselves too thin and allow themselves to get bogged down in trivial tasks for which they are ill-suited. The result? They don't have enough remaining bandwidth to focus on the true essentials.

Identify your "Top 20" activities and focus as much time and energy on them as possible. Delegate, outsource or delete everything else! Don't be the choke point in you own business.

★ ★ ★ ★ ★ ★ ★ ★ ★ ★ ★ ★ ★ ★ ★ ★

So far, we've focused on forming new teams. What if you already have a team of people around you? The exact same principles apply.

Start by having each key team member take the _StrengthsFinder 2.0_ and _Kolbe A Index_ assessment, at a minimum. We recommend using a Certified Kolbe Consultant to analyze the Kolbe results, particularly if you have a large team (see the resource section on our companion website at **www.VictorySuccessResources.com** for more information). The results will give you keen insight into where your team is strong and where adjustments, realignment or new hires are necessary.

A common finding is some existing team members aren't a great fit for their current positions. You may need to realign their responsibilities, move them to a different position, or place them within a different internal team. If they can't or won't make the adjustments to better align the team, it's time for them to go. As before, make sure you follow your SOP and document all interactions with team members.

It's always painful to let people go, especially if they've been with you for a while. But sometimes it's the only way to get your organization running on all cylinders and achieve peak performance. We also find that team members who aren't a good fit in your company aren't going to be happy. When you cut them loose, you free them to find work in a place that's a better fit for them.

You are the Maestro and it's your job to conduct the rest of the team for maximum effectiveness

Your goal in building and/or adjusting your team is to free you to do the things you do well...the things you are passionate about... the things that make money. For the majority of Vetrepreneurs®, these are also the critical revenue generating tasks most profitable for your business. Focus on the 3 to 5 areas where you shine, such as making the sales pitch, managing the relationships, networking with key decision makers, creating unique content or providing strategic direction for the rest of the team.

You are the maestro and it's your job as the leader of your organization to conduct the rest of the team for maximum effectiveness. Make it a priority to delegate or outsource anything you don't do well, or really dislike doing, and empower your team to take care of everything else.

None of this happens with the wave of a magic wand. It will take some time to hire the right people and make the necessary adjustments to get your team running on all cylinders. Once you have everything humming along at peak efficiency, how do you sustain that momentum?

The best way we know to accomplish this is making sure the entire team stays focused on the shared vision and goals of the organization. Keep the vision front and center. Develop a vision statement and make sure that it makes sense to your team. Clearly communicate your vision to your team on a regular basis; explain where you are going as an organization and why you are going there. When people have a clear picture of your larger vision, it's much easier for them to buy into it. Otherwise, your people end up working on unconnected pieces of a puzzle, without knowing what that puzzle should look like.

Team members will get frustrated when they don't see how their activities fit into the larger picture. Strongly consider regular weekly team meetings to share what's going on, recognize team members for outstanding performance, and answer questions. You can do it in person, over the phone, with a video message, or use a service like Skype if you have a virtual or geographically dispersed team.

Best of all, it doesn't need to take long—maybe 30 minutes tops— and it really keeps people engaged. Lay out the key goals for the week and big events coming up in the near future. Don't be afraid to lay a vexing challenge on the table and ask for solutions.

When you hire good people, allow them some freedom to

maneuver. Give them the mission parameters: the goal, the timeline for completion, and any key touch points along the line. Empower them with the authority and autonomy necessary to succeed and then get out of the way! Let your team take over. Let them implement strategies to get everything done. Give them permission for a "touch and go" if they have questions or need clarification. Other than that, let them know you trust them to accomplish the goal.

Having a team like this frees you from the constant worry about things getting done, that slows down so many entrepreneurs. This is exciting, invigorating and freeing because it allows you to follow your passion and stay connected with why you became an entrepreneur in the first place!

The main ingredient to stardom is the rest of the team.
—*John Wooden, Legendary Basketball Coach*

Million Dollar Minute

Take a sheet of paper, and divide it into 3 columns. Title the first column: Doing, the second column: Great At, and the third column: Love It. In the Doing column, list all of the things you are doing in your business at the moment. In the Great At column, list all of the things you are doing that you are great at. In the Love It column, write down the things you are doing that you love to do.

Circle the items you listed in both the Great At and Love It columns. Those are the activities on which you need to concentrate. They are most likely the areas of your business you are best at, and most passionate about. As for the other items on your list, they are wasting your time. Either delegate or eliminate them, and get busy doing the things that you do best!

For a template to assist you in completing this **Million Dollar Minute**, please visit our website at **www.VictorySuccessResources.com**.

OPS

★ ★ ★ ★ ★ ★ ★ ★ ★ ★ ★ ★ ★ ★ ★ ★ ★ ★

If you find yourself in a fair fight, you didn't plan your operation properly.
—*Colonel David Hackworth*

Key Challenge

Many MVEs fail to create clear, easy to implement and repeatable systems within their businesses or, if developed, fail to employ them consistently. Not having proper systems in place from start–up forward prevents growth, lowers the value of the business to a potential future buyer and can ultimately lead to the utter failure of the business.

Leaders win through logistics. Vision, sure. Strategy, yes. But when you go to war, you need to have both toilet paper and bullets at the right place at the right time. In other words, you must win through superior logistics.
—*Tom Peters, USN Vietnam Veteran (1966-1970)*
Best-selling author of In Search of Excellence

Operations?
We Don't Need No Stinking Operations!

They aren't sexy or exciting, but certain operations are critical in order for your business to survive, let alone thrive. First, let's define what we mean by operations. Operations are ongoing, repeatable activities that keep your business running smoothly. These activities include financial systems, sales lead generation and follow-through, inventory management, customer service, routine strategic planning and anything else that your business repeats with any regularity throughout the year. In other words, operations encompasses just about everything you do to keep your business going!

Most MVEs find working on the systems of their business about as exciting as watching paint dry, and prefer concentrating on the "fun stuff" like interacting with customers or developing strategic vision. Just like Intel, developing systems, especially in the early stages of your business, can feel like endless drudgery. However, just like Intel, the effort that leads to well-refined systems is vital to creating sustainable success.

Why are systems so important? Think of it this way: A soldier on the battlefield doesn't get to the front lines by himself and he has no chance of success if he tries to fight alone. In addition to the other soldiers around him, he has a team of supporting personnel: specialists who gather, interpret and disseminate intel, logisticians who work the supply lines from point of origin all the way to the foxhole, and communications experts who ensure maximum combat power is brought to bear with synchronicity. Without these systems functioning effectively in the background, the front line soldier doesn't have much hope for survival, not to mention success.

Far too many vetrepreneurs lack even the "bare bones" skeleton of systemized operations

Think of operations as those support systems that enable your success. They are a necessary part of doing battle in the business world. Unfortunately, we see far too many vetrepreneurs who lack even the "bare bones" skeleton of systemized operations. They may have an idea about how they should do things or even have it well mapped out in their heads, but they don't have an Ops Manual that details, in writing, the various processes of the business.

You need a basic understanding of every department and function of your organization. The more complex your operation grows, the harder it is for you to know every detail of what's happening. Greater complexity means you won't be an expert on everything, but the systems you put in place will provide a working understanding of all the moving parts in your business.

★ ★ ★ ★ ★ ★ ★ ★ ★ ★ ★ ★ ★ ★ ★ ★

Intel Insight

Systems Aren't Sexy, But...

They don't get a lot of notoriety or front-page press and this is why many vetrepreneurs tend to ignore them. We MVEs desire to go out and achieve (which isn't a bad thing). We want to be the hotshot fighter pilot tearing up the sky in the F/A-18 Super Hornet. We want to mix it up, engage the enemy in an exciting dogfight and deliver the goods on time and on target. For most of us, dealing with this systems stuff isn't very exciting.

But we know the pilot never gets off the deck without the support staff and systems. Everyone, from the mechanic who keeps the plane in flying condition, to the people who deliver fuel to the air base or aircraft carrier, to the factory where the bombs are made, has a hand in making the mission a success. If just one of them fails to perform, the mission fails. Your systems are the equivalent of the support a hotshot pilot gets. They allow you to do the things you really want to. Ignore them and you will end up in serious trouble!

You may be thinking, "Why is this so important...? As long as I am growing sales and bringing in money, won't the back office stuff just take care of itself?" We wish that were so! Unfortunately, we also know from painful personal experience that trying to operate any company, from a solo professional practice to a large multi-site organization with high complexity, is akin to wandering through a dense minefield with a blindfold on. Sooner or later, you are going to step on something very unpleasant with potentially disastrous results!

The good news? The benefits from taking the time and energy to create, implement and occasionally tweak systems are legion. Systemized operations result in greater profits, better customer service, more targeted marketing efforts, stronger team management and ultimately, a significantly more valuable company should you try to sell it as part of your exit strategy.

Let's look at a prime example that all successful entrepreneurs experience—the "Big Sale." A large bolus of money from a major contract hits the top line, but actual profit turns out far lower than you anticipated. Where did the money go? For MVEs without effective cash flow systems, the usual answer is "I have no idea!"

Without good systems in place, the money leeches will eventually bleed you dry

When you have clear, repeatable systems in place for handling money as it comes in, you can track exactly where money goes in your company. For instance, you might find a hidden "money leech" in the form of unnecessary expenses, higher than expected travel costs or outsourcing over-rides that siphon away your profit. With the right system in place, you can quickly ID the leech and pour some strategic salt on it. Without good systems in place, the money leeches will eventually bleed you dry!

Solid systems are also a great way to reinforce gaps in your skill set or inherent strengths, freeing you to focus your energy to where you are strongest. Let's say you are great at getting the client to "yes" and closing the sales, if you can get in front of the client, but you aren't terribly strong in managing lead generation or sales call follow-up. Will you occasionally land a deal without a good system in place? Sure, but how much more effective will you be with a good lead generation system combined with a highly automated follow-up system?

Such a system, which can easily be run by a virtual team member with the right skill set, frees you to focus on your "core 20 percent" of highest and best time/energy use. Your team and supporting systems generate the leads, set-up the appointment, provide the pertinent pre-meeting intel and initiate the post-call, follow-up system based on the outcome of the initial meeting. You are now free of the constant struggle of front and back end sales cycle management and free to tackle more valuable strategic projects.

The long-term result? Greater revenue, more profits, a well-functioning team and a happy MVE who isn't stuck in the weeds. You spend your time working ON the business, not IN the business. Sounds pretty good, right?

It is pretty good, but there is still that pesky short term challenge of putting time and effort into building these systems on the front-end. We won't lie to you, it's not easy for most MVEs to get past the initial inertia for putting these critical systems into place. The good news is others have already done much of the work for you (more on that later) and the benefits of having these systems in place far surpass the temporary inconvenience of creating them.

One of the best reasons for systemizing as many aspects of your business as possible is that it allows you to concentrate on building a business that adds value to people's lives: your clients/customers, your team members, your family and ultimately, yours. Too many entrepreneurs spend all their time heads down, working under the hood, treating their companies as "just the place I work" instead of building something with lasting significance. We think it's important for MVEs beginning their companies to spend a bit of time thinking about the end game; their exit strategy.

If you are currently in business and someone walked up to you on the street and offered you ten times revenue (a very generous offer) to purchase your business lock, stock and barrel on the condition it was a turnkey operation—all ready to go—would you be ready? Are the systems running in your company right now robust enough for a new owner to quickly understand the way the business works? For most of us, the answer is no. Yet these systems need to be in place, clearly

defined and well understood by key people in your organization—
even if you have no plans to sell!

Finally, effective systems provide you freedom, since you can step
away for a week or even a month and be confident that the business will
be able to run smoothly and produce revenue even while you're gone.
The earlier you start systemizing, the easier it is to keep everything
under control, so don't put it off! In the next section, we will share
some tips on how to systemize your operations and delve deeper into
the benefits of starting today.

> *The best time to plant a tree is 20 years ago.*
> *The next best time is now!*
> —*Chinese Proverb*

The Time To Start Is Now

The best time to do the right thing in your business is as soon as
possible. We strongly encourage our start-up coaching clients to
build their business systems starting on Day One. Those running an
established business obviously can't start from the beginning, but they
can start today. Avoid trying to get caught up on old data and filing
systems before implementing your new systems, this will only slow
you down. Instead, get the new system in place, and use some of the
time created by the new efficiencies to address legacy issues over time.

So where do you begin? Each business is unique, so we can't give
you absolute specifics on every system that your company needs.
However, there are three critical areas for which you must commit to
developing good operations.

The first area is cash flow. We cannot stress enough the importance
of understanding your cash flow. At the most basic level, you need to

know how much money comes in and where it goes. Unfortunately, many of the vetrepreneurs we connect with don't have a firm handle on their cash flow. They may have a ballpark idea of how much is coming in the front door, but possess no clarity around where it goes afterwards and don't have a clue whether it's being spent effectively or not.

For example, say you don't have a system to track where your customers come from or how they find you. This means you can't tell which of the seven forms of advertising you are using works the best. If you add a single question, "How did you hear about us?," to your intake process, you might discover 90 percent of your new business comes from just 2 of the 7 advertising channels. Tracking this allows you to understand the best deployment strategy for your advertising dollars, jettison the dead weight methods, and shift resources to your key promotional channels.

Cash flow systems also allow you to keep accurate records, which is always very important at tax time. Obviously, you want to avoid trouble with local, state and federal tax agencies for failing to properly handle income or payroll taxes. At the same time, you want to ensure that you are taking advantage of all legitimate deductions.

The second area is what we term "professional operations." Many MVEs unwittingly expose themselves to unnecessary legal liability. You might be using decade-old contracts with outdated language or be out of compliance with required local, state or federal regulatory requirements for your industry.

Regular check-ups with a legal advisor can easily confirm whether or not you are in compliance with any new laws, using up-to-date documents and availing yourself of the best business entity to ensure adequate legal protections. Without the correct system in place, the check-ups won't happen and these items could easily fall through the cracks. Often, you don't find out there's a problem until you get sued. You might be completely innocent, but still end up paying the price because you don't have the right legal protections or insurance. You also need a system to ensure any other business with which you enter into a joint venture with is up-to-date on all of these things as well. Otherwise, you could be liable if you are working on a joint project and they get sued!

The third area is personnel. Key questions to consider around your personnel system include:

★ What is your hiring process?
★ How do you determine the qualifications for each position?
★ What is your probation or introduction period?
★ How do you conduct performance reviews?
★ How do you put together compensation packages?

Your personnel systems should also answer questions about job performance. How will you determine whether a certain position is bringing value to your organization? Many companies have no system in place to measure this.

It's daunting to think about building all these different systems from scratch. Fortunately, if you invest some exploratory intel time, you'll discover many of the systems you need already exist and are successfully supporting businesses just like yours. Examples include:

★ Computer systems
★ Specialized software programs
★ Human resources manuals
★ Consulting agreement templates

★ Virtual call centers to answer your phone with a live, human voice
★ Client relationship management (CRM) systems
★ Sales lead generation and management systems

In fact, about 90–95 percent of the systems that you need to start or grow your business are available "off the shelf" and require little or no customization. You and/or your team will need to put some time in tweaking the last few pieces specific to your business.

The vast majority of what you need is already available

We routinely see vetrepreneurs get overwhelmed and spend way too much time, energy and money trying to reinvent the wheel. This approach is exhausting and unnecessary, so don't do it! Talk to others in your industry to see what he/she are using, reach out to your coach or mentor to see what they recommend, and hire a knowledgeable consultant for 1–2 hours to draft a strategic systems plan. Trust us, the vast majority of what you need is already available—you just need to invest some properly channeled time and energy to find it.

Another costly long-term error that we see many MVEs make is automatically defaulting to the lowest cost version available for each system they implement. While understandable, since it costs money to purchase software or hire a systems consultant, this poverty mindset can really hurt you in the long run. Before finalizing your purchase decision, ask yourself these questions:

★ "How much money am I willing to waste by NOT having the right systems in place?"

★ "How much time am I going to throw away doing the same things over again?"

★ "How much will I lose if I open myself up to a lawsuit because my contracts aren't up to date?"

Remember, developing, purchasing and implementing the right systems is an investment in your business, not an expense. In addition, enormous strides are taking place almost daily in scalable, highly customizable technology solutions that allow you to run most businesses from anywhere in the world with a smartphone, a laptop and a reliable internet connection (please visit the **Resources** section of our companion website **www.VictorySuccessResources.com** for current information on our favorite solutions).

We place so much emphasis on getting good systems in place early because we have learned the hard way how costly it is not to have them, and the opportunities that open up once they are in place. We will explore these opportunities in the next section.

I am tempted to make a slightly exaggerated statement:
that logistics is all of war-making, except shooting the guns,
releasing the bombs, and firing the torpedoes.
—Admiral Lynde D. McCormick, United States Navy

Good Systems Create Great Opportunities

A primary reason most MVEs go into business is to create a good life for their families. Earlier in the chapter, we shared how systems will make you more profitable, enabling you to track your cash flow and eliminate the money leeches draining your profits. We also shared how automating systems will save you substantial time in the long run. The end result? Systems actually allow you to enjoy that better life with your family instead of spending it at the office!

Let's step back and look at the bigger picture for a moment. Pardon us for being morbid, but what would happen if you weren't around to run your business? If a bus hit you tomorrow, would your business grind to a halt? For many vetrepreneurs, the answer is "yes." If the intimate knowledge of how your business runs is locked up in your brain, then no one else can truly make your business work. You can have the best team in the world, but if they have to come to you for all the answers, they are dead in the water the minute that you're not around.

Without documented, repeatable systems in place, whoever steps in to run your company is at a serious disadvantage. Imagine your spouse or children trying to pick up the pieces and keep your company going. Obviously, you want to provide them with every opportunity to succeed. In this worst-case scenario, good systems are one way you provide for your family—even after you're gone!

> *They [systems] maximize the value of your company in the event that someone wants to buy it*

But let's assume you will be around for a long time. The best way to take advantage of opportunities that may come your way is to have effective systems in place. Why? They maximize the value of your company in the event that someone wants to buy it. You can seriously undercut the value of your company by not implementing good systems.

Systems that exist only in your head aren't very attractive to buyers. Some will shy away from companies that don't have systems in place.

Others will make lowball offers for your business, because of the extra risk involved in buying a company with anemic systems. If part of your exit plan is to sell your company, it is absolutely critical that you create and maintain superior systems.

★ ★ ★ ★ ★ ★ ★ ★ ★ ★ ★ ★ ★ ★ ★ ★

Intel Insight

Your Company is Worthless
Phil Dyer, CFP®, RLP®, CPCC
America's Entrepreneur Strategist

A recent white paper took the financial planning industry by storm. Authored by industry leader Mark Hurley, CEO of Fiduciary Network, the paper boldly stated that 95 percent of the nearly 20,000 financial planning firms nationwide had virtually no intrinsic sale value. The primary reason? No systems!

The "value" of these companies (many of them 20 to 30 years old) resides in the expertise of the owners and their teams. Unfortunately, they've made little or no attempt to turn that expertise into systems that other people can use successfully. There are no written procedures. The people in the company aren't cross-trained to do each other's jobs, meaning no one has the big picture of what the company does, only their own small puzzle piece. Therefore, if the owner or his team leaves, there's no way to keep the business going without a lot of time, effort and expense on the part of the new owner.

This challenge is very common for service businesses. They start small, as 1-2 person operations, and grow in spurts with little or no strategic planning. Ad hoc systems are thrown into the mix as the company grows, usually in response to a crisis, but nothing is ever documented and even the simple tasks can become convoluted, multi-step processes that make no sense to anyone but the owner. You don't want to be one of those businesses!

★ ★ ★ ★ ★ ★ ★ ★ ★ ★ ★ ★ ★ ★ ★ ★ ★

Understanding the value of systems is just as important if you plan to purchase an existing company. Ensure that you fully investigate the organization's systems from top to bottom. If you find out there's nothing under the hood, either walk away or negotiate a deeply discounted price. Also, make sure the purchase agreement you sign stipulates that you are buying all the systems that come with that company. If needed, negotiate that the previous owner (or other key personnel) stays on board for a set period of time, to train you in the essential systems for the business. The previous owner can stay for a week, a month, or whatever period of time you believe necessary. The main thing is that you understand the systems of that business so you can hit the ground running!

Intel Insight

Poor Systems Decisions Can Kill Your Business
—Larry Broughton
Founder/CEO of Broughton Hospitality Group

I once sold a hotel to a woman who had made a lot of money in a big real estate deal. That one deal made her an "expert" (at least in her mind) and she approached the deal with an "I already know everything" attitude. During the negotiations, I offered her all the systems that went with the property—the website, the reservation system and the pictography. Her response? "I don't need any of that...I don't want any of it."

I strongly encouraged—almost begged—her to take the systems as part of the business. But she just as adamantly refused. I don't know if she simply didn't understand how critical the in-place systems were, or if she just had bad advisors around her. What I do know is that she lost money on the hotel. She eventually sold the hotel for less than she bought it.

Learn from her mistake. Make sure you buy the systems that control the operation of the company. If you find that a company you want to buy does not have those systems in place, that company is worth much, much less. It's going to take a lot more work—and money—for you to get it up to speed.

Million Dollar Minute

Look back at Column 1 of the 3-Column Exercise in the previous chapter. Find the task item that you like the least or procrastinate on the most. This is an ideal target for systemization. Decide what you want the outcome to be and how you can delegate, delete or outsource to achieve that desired outcome.

RAPID ACTION

★ ★ ★ ★ ★ ★ ★ ★ ★ ★ ★ ★ ★ ★ ★ ★ ★ ★ ★ ★

A good plan violently executed today is better
than a perfect plan next week.
—*General George S. Patton, Jr.*

Success Comes To Doers, Not Dreamers

We've all heard the expression, "Knowledge is power." It's an old saying and many people believe it. Unfortunately, there's one small problem; it's a lie. Don't believe it for a second. The truth is that action is power. You can hook your brain up to the Library of Congress and download every bit of information residing there, and it won't do you a bit of good until you act on that knowledge.

Action delivers results. Action creates opportunities. Action dampens potential fall-out from the occasional (but inevitable) error. Taking rapid, decisive action is the single greatest differentiator between barely surviving and truly thriving.

History shines with the exploits of leaders who took decisive action, including: Alexander the Great, Julius Caesar, Saladin, Frederick the Great, Horatio Nelson, Napoleon Bonaparte, Robert E. Lee, Gregory Zhukov and George S. Patton, Jr. Their exploits overshadowed the so-called leaders whose vacillation, dithering and endless indecision turned them into historical footnotes, such as: Darius III of Persia, Publius Varus, Horatio Gates, Antonio Lopez De Santa Anna, George B. McClellan, Ambrose Burnside, Douglas Haig and Maurice Gamelin.

We can't over stress the importance of taking rapid action. We see too many vetrepreneurs who are in a holding pattern, waiting for just the right opportunity, waiting for just a little more information, waiting to finish the formal business plan or adding the last touches to the website, waiting for the perfect alignment of the stars. They wait six months, nine months, even a year or more, stuck in a holding pattern. Something prevents them from shifting out of neutral, taking action and moving forward.

We know top achievers in many different industries. Men and women who create positive change, run great organizations, experience explosive growth, and are continually innovating. They share few common exterior traits: They have different heights, weights, ethnicities, political leanings and education levels. The single salient strength that ties top achievers together is getting things done!

The ability to take rapid, decisive action, is more important than intelligence, education and raw talent. In many ways, it is the single best predictor of the level of success that you will achieve, both in business and in life.

We often find MVEs sitting at the starting line idling because they are waiting on some external factor, such as the government approving a big contract, the bank finalizing a financing package or a team member finishing a proposal. They fixate completely on clearing this one perceived hurdle to moving their business forward and everything grinds to a halt.

You must take action in your business and life because, quite frankly, nobody owes you anything. This includes the government, your employer, your clients/customers and your spouse or significant other. No one else will solve your problems, so sitting around waiting for your ship to come in is futile. The only way to solve a challenge, create or take advantage of an opportunity and ultimately reach your goals, is to get in gear and take action.

Sound a bit harsh? Good…it's meant to! Please don't confuse our "nobody owes you anything" comment above with operating the Lone Wolf way. It's easy to overlay the two, but the most common action step we recommend when mentoring a "stuck" MVE, is engaging outside help to shift perspective and reframe the challenge.

We celebrate dreamers in our culture. The self-help shelves at bookstores are packed with titles directing us to follow our dreams. We get it, which is why Chapter One focuses on **Vision**. Dreamers create transformative ideas that lead to great advancements in every area of business and life. That said, dreaming alone isn't enough and any cursory study of leading change agents reveals they take decisive action to turn dreams into reality.

If you get lazy as an entrepreneur, you end up with no food on the table

Vetrepreneurs must be doers as well as dreamers. This transition is difficult when coming from a W-2 paycheck environment, where you receive a regular paycheck even if you aren't working all that hard to earn it. Sometimes when you're in a "safe" corporate or government job, it's easy to get a bit lazy (we know, we've been there personally). As an entrepreneurs don't have the luxury to slack off; your income relates directly to the amount of positive activity in which you engage. If you get lazy as an entrepreneur, you end up with no food on the table!

Intel Insight

System Shock

A big shock for most MVEs is the sheer volume of information, issues and challenges they must deal with in the normal course of running their business. Whether you are starting up straight out of the military, or are making the shift from post military corporate or government employment, it's unlikely that you currently deal with the myriad responsibilities that come with entrepreneurship. These changes require a completely different mindset, and also explain why getting stuck is so easy!

It really takes a whole new mindset and it will probably take time until you hit your entrepreneurial stride. When you stumble or even fall, fight the urge to get too down on yourself or allow negative self-talk to creep in. Being a vetrepreneur is tough enough without constantly beating yourself up!

When we say, "take action," we aren't just referring to initiating projects and activities. Completing actions, closing the loop and crossing them off you to do list is crucial. This is a major challenge for many MVEs who are great idea generators, but not as strong on the idea completion front. Entrepreneurs in general suffer from the "bright shiny object" syndrome...it's part of our DNA (we know this intimately as charter members of the Bright Shiny Object Club).

Ever start one project and pursue it with boundless energy until another bright shiny object catches your eye and distracts you? You then dive into that project until the next shiny object surfaces. The result? It's very easy to build an impressive portfolio of brilliant, but half-completed projects, and never actually accomplish anything!

This pattern poses several significant dangers. First, these partial projects are seldom profitable and each represents a lost opportunity for income, building credibility in your industry or making your business more efficient. We know way too many vetrepreneurs whose careers consist of one unrealized opportunity after another because they don't push any one opportunity over the finish line.

Each unfinished task siphons off some of your cognitive ability

The second danger is what we call "entrepreneurial brain drain." Each unfinished activity creates what researchers term an "open loop" in your mind. You keep thinking about an unfinished task, even when you are working on something else. Each unfinished task siphons off some of your cognitive ability, creates background noise in your subconscious, and lowers your ability to focus on your current project. The more open loops from unfinished projects, the greater the brain drain and noise level. Eventually, this effect may completely short-circuit your ability get stuff done!

The best way to avoid entrepreneurial brain drain is to complete one task before moving to the next. Easier said than done, given the modern propensity for multi-tasking, but making this shift can have a huge impact on your productivity, as you bring maximum brain firepower to bear on a task before moving on. Taking action is essential; completing those actions is even more important to your long-term success.

If you aren't accustomed to taking action, if you are more comfortable thinking, pondering, and contemplating until the spirit moves you, then developing an action-oriented mindset will seem strange at first. But you will grow into it. Ever go out for a run after a long exercise layoff? The first time is often very uncomfortable. Your legs hurt, you can barely breathe, and you're sore the next day. If you keep moving, however, your muscles adapt, your lung capacity increases, and soon you are stronger because of the effort you put into running.

The same thing happens when you start taking action. You may feel awkward or unprepared at first as you move out towards your goals and achieve success, but you will get more comfortable. Every success, and lessons learned from the occasional failure, increases your confidence and comfort level with taking decisive action. Soon, you will discover that you possess a different mindset, an action-oriented mindset.

This action-oriented mindset is a huge component of your success! But what do you do if you are primed for action, but unsure which action to take? That's what the next section is all about.

No battle plan survives contact with the enemy intact.
—General Helmuth von Moltke the Elder
Chief of the Prussian General Staff (1857-1887)

Taking Action In The Face Of Uncertainty

Wouldn't it be great if you had a clearly defined target and perfect sight picture in mind each time before you took action? Unfortunately, today's dynamic business battlefield offers few perfect looks or sure things. We've already shared how waiting for perfect alignment is a direct route to the poor house, so you must develop some comfort level with moving out and taking course corrective action as you go forward.

Of course, you aren't taking action blindly. Following the principles we've already laid out, we trust you've applied some brainpower to:

★ Developing the vision for your organization
★ Researching and analyzing appropriate Intel
★ Connecting with coaches/mentors
★ Building your custom-designed support team
★ Getting the right systems in place to support your growth

At some point though, you must stop analyzing and start doing! We talk to far too many MVEs that are trapped in "analysis paralysis," struggling to get into action. They have reams of information and multiple courses of action swirling around in their heads, but don't know what to do with it. Trying to pick the right target when you are stuck in entrepreneurial overwhelm sucks, quite frankly. We've been there multiple times in our extensive business careers.

★ ★ ★ ★ ★ ★ ★ ★ ★ ★ ★ ★ ★ ★ ★ ★

Intel Insight

The Perfect Time For Action

We'd like to ask a simple question. Is now the perfect time to take action? Absolutely not! There's no such thing as the perfect time to do anything. Perfectionism is the mortal enemy of the entrepreneur and those that attempt to attain it end up mighty frustrated. Even if you manage to craft the perfect plan and arrange perfect circumstances, they only remain perfect while on paper. It starts breaking down the moment you implement and make contact with external forces. Check the quote at the top of this section, "No battle plan survives contact with the enemy intact."

This is just as true in business as in war. You will need to improvise, adapt and take course-corrective action. You might need a small course adjustment of 5 to 10 degrees, or a complete U-turn. Figure it out in stride and keep moving. If you stop every ten feet to reanalyze everything, others will fly past you in terms of success.

They may not be as smart as or well-educated as you. They may not have your network, or financial backing or support systems. Their product or service might not be anywhere near as good as yours. But if they have developed the habit of rapid action and are continuously moving forward, they will consistently beat you to market and co-opt your clients/ customers. All because they initiated their imperfect plan and took decisive action!

So what should you do? Our advice is to simply get moving! Connect with your vision, goals and Intel to determine the initial direction and get rolling. Focus your marketing on those you believe are most interested in your product or service (just remember, target what they want, not what you think they need). Look for low hanging fruit and take on targets of opportunity as you go. People are often surprised at how easily clients/customers appear once they get into action.

As you're rolling, take note of what's working and what isn't. Refine your message or shift your market to zero in on your most receptive audience, and discard pre-conceived notions that don't pan out. This "build the airplane as you fly" approach is incredibly uncomfortable for some vetrepreneurs, but is critically important, especially if you are in start-up or rapid growth mode.

This approach is the business equivalent of recon by fire. In combat, when a unit believes a certain area is a likely enemy position, the unit may open fire on that position, hoping to provoke a reaction from the enemy. As an entrepreneur, sometimes you must do exactly the same thing. If you believe you can successfully compete in a market segment, you need to engage and open fire on that segment (figuratively speaking, of course).

Engaging the market can take many forms, depending on your resources, skill set, support team and the market itself. Focused (and low-cost) marketing, speaking appearances, and joint ventures with a complimentary business already enjoying success in the market are all solid strategies. If you are correct and it's a target-rich environment, your message will start resonating and gaining traction, allowing you to expand your business.

★ ★ ★ ★ ★ ★ ★ ★ ★ ★ ★ ★ ★ ★ ★ ★

Intel Insight

What if I'm Wrong?

We believe the fear of making mistakes is one of the biggest reasons that entrepreneurs restrain themselves from taking action. It shouldn't be; failure is an important ingredient of success. This may sound counter-intuitive, but it's absolutely true. When you fail in business, and you will fail, it simply means you tried something that didn't work. Learn from the mistake, make adjustments and try again. Most highly successful entrepreneurs freely admit they learned far more from their failures than from their successes.

For an MVE, failure in business shouldn't cause too much fear. After all, on the battlefield, a mistake can cost lives. Fortunately, business is rarely a life or death affair. You might lose some money, some respect, or a little dignity; you can recover from all of those. So look at failure for what it really is, the opportunity to learn and expand your knowledge.

In reality, fear of failure is misplaced fear. The only thing you should fear is inaction. You can recover from mistakes. You can regroup, analyze what went wrong and make course corrections. But if you do nothing, we guarantee you'll miss every opportunity for success that comes your way. We don't want you looking back over your life and wondering, "What might have happened if only I had done...?"

Letting fear hold you back can easily become a habit. The good news is that learning to take action is also a habit. Habits are like muscles. Muscles don't start out strong and you don't just wake up one morning and decide to bench press 300 pounds. You work your muscles vigorously and consistently, and before long you notice the difference in your strength level.

Your "action habit muscle" operates under the same principle. It may not be strong right now, but the more you exercise it, the stronger it becomes. For most of us, the hardest part of any exercise program is getting started. We will share 3 simple exercises in the next section to help you quickly strengthen your action habit muscles.

Remember, fortune favors those who take action. You will find opportunity by moving out and staying true to your vision and values, even if it's not the kind you originally expected. We know scores of MVEs who started moving down the entrepreneurial road with one concept and discovered a far more lucrative opportunity right around the first bend.

Action creates and attracts opportunities

Unfortunately, we also know a fair number that just sit on the road, convinced of the brilliance of their own ideas and waiting for business to come to them. No amount of positive thinking or self-affirmation will cause opportunities to fall from the sky and drop into your lap (no matter what the Law of Attraction says). Action creates and attracts opportunities.

You may be thinking, "Great, guys…I get that I need to develop an action mindset, but how? How do I go from analysis paralysis and fear of failure to moving forward and making the vision for my company a reality?"

We're glad you asked! In the next section, we give you three simple tools to get you, and keep you, in action.

I never worry about action, but inaction.
—*Sir Winston Churchill*

Develop An Action Mindset

During our military careers, we both had the opportunity to jump out of perfectly good airplanes. Of course, the military doesn't just take you up in a plane and throw you out. You go through the proper training and have the right equipment. You build your confidence through a series of small successes until you are ready for that first jump. Then the green light comes on, you shuffle to the door of the C-130 and you...freeze. Despite all the training, preparation and previous successes, you still freeze.

In a combat situation, if you don't jump at the right time, the results can be disastrous. You (and everyone behind you) could miss the drop zone. Your unit might become separated. You could even end up landing right on an enemy position instead of your drop zone. That's why there's a kind, gentle jumpmaster in the plane to shove you out the door if necessary.

For this section, we will be your jumpmasters—getting you out the door and into action with 3 simple exercises. We've touched on these concepts throughout the chapter, and they are crucial for getting into action. Let's dive in!

★ **Action Exercise #1—Go for Progress, Not Perfection:** Understand, accept and internalize the fact that there is no perfect plan. Even your most meticulous plans won't survive contact on the business battlefield, so stop trying to be perfect! Get moving in the direction of making your vision a reality and keep your head up, looking for opportunities. Strive for steady progress and make course corrections as needed through the filters of your vision, your mentors and your team.

Today's business is so dynamic that the only constant is change. Technology, market and economic conditions, new applications for existing products/services, and the wants of clients and customers are always in motion. To succeed, you must be moving too!

★ **Action Exercise #2—Don't Try to Eat the Elephant in One Bite:** We often fail to take action because the task before us seems too daunting, like trying to eat an entire elephant in one sitting. The solution? Try breaking seemingly overwhelming tasks into smaller chunks and dig into the bite-sized pieces with gusto! Once you start knocking out the smaller pieces, you'll find the big task looks much less menacing.

Also, don't be afraid to start with something small. Sometimes, just doing something relatively simple, like making a phone call to schedule an appointment with a potential client, gives you the motivation you need to attack the larger project. Action fuels motivation!

★ **Action Exercise #3—The More You Act, the Easier It Gets:** Developing your "action habit muscle" is just like any other exercise in building strength or cardiovascular endurance. The more you take action, the stronger you become and the easier it becomes.

This is the primary reason that breaking overwhelming tasks into bite-sized pieces works so well. You accomplish one small task, and then another and then another. Before long, you'll notice you are thinking differently and actively looking for new reasons and ways to act, instead of making excuses for why you can't.

Use these 3 simple exercises any time you feel yourself getting stuck or frustrated. Remember: Aim for progress, not perfection—break big projects into bite-sized pieces—the more you practice taking rapid, decisive action, the easier it becomes.

NOW MOVE OUT!

Million Dollar Minute

In **Action Exercise #2** above, we recommend breaking overwhelming tasks into bite-size chunks. One of the oldest, simplest, and most effective, tools ever developed for getting things done is the humble "To-Do List."

Its power is underestimated, which is why few achievement and success *seekers* use it. Ask top *achievers* about the importance of a To-Do List, however, and you'll find few who can live without one. Just beware of getting overly enthusiastic about adding items to your list. It's easy to feel overwhelmed and drained by too many tasks, which can lead to procrastination.

Develop a list of all the items that you need to complete in order to achieve your goals. Then, review your list and identify the TOP two or three projects that need your attention right away. Break these top items down into smaller, actionable items that you can complete in the next 24-36 hours. Each time you complete a task, cross it off your list. Feels good, doesn't it?

Continually review your list. Ask yourself if you need to do *everything* on the list. Can you delegate anything on there?

Put new items on a new to-do list. This list will be far less scary, making it easier to take action, and get things done.

Visit **www.VictorySuccessResources.com** for sample to-do lists and tools to help you take rapid action today!

YOU

★ ★ ★ ★ ★ ★ ★ ★ ★ ★ ★ ★ ★ ★ ★ ★ ★ ★ ★ ★

In reading the lives of great men, I found that the first victory they won
was over themselves...self-discipline with all of them came first.
—President Harry S. Truman

It's All About You

The first six principles we gave you: Vision, Intel, Coaching, Team, Ops and Rapid Action, are essential elements of building long-term success in business. But unless you apply the ideas in this chapter, the other principles won't matter. When you strip everything else away, your success—in your business and in your life—depends on you!

Think of the other principles as spokes in a wheel. You are the hub of that wheel. No matter how strong the spokes are, the wheel will eventually fall apart if the hub isn't sound. In this chapter we'll share our perspectives on what it takes to build a business, and a life, of long-lasting significance.

When you strip away everything else, your success—
in business and in life—depends on you

Why do you want to live the vetrepreneur lifestyle? At the most basic level, of course, the majority of us desire to create a stream of income that supports the kind of life we want for our family and ourselves. Most of us want to support charities and causes that we believe in. Finally, many of us want to use our experience and talents to leave the world better than how we found it.

When you look at the sacrifice and dedication it takes to successfully start and grow a small business, you know there is more involved than just making a living. After all, you are signing up for a roller-coaster ride of ups and downs, victories and defeats, frustration and euphoria and most of these come before 0900 each morning!

Why? What drives us to do what we do? The assessment tools that we discussed earlier in the book (*StrengthsFinders 2.0* and the *Kolbe A Index*) are great starting places for figuring out what motivates you.

This also ties into the vision you have for your organization, as well as your personal vision for your life. Review your company and personal vision statements regularly. In fact, take a few moments and review them right now. If you haven't developed them yet, take 5 minutes and jot down some thoughts. Remember, vision is not something that you think about once and then hide away in your desk drawer. Keep the reasons you do what you do front and center and refer to them often, especially when things get tough.

Intel Insight

Clarity is Attractive

You should clearly communicate who you are and what you stand for to your potential customers. It will resonate with many of them, and your company will be much more attractive because of it.

Could you potentially scare some customers off by talking about your values? Perhaps. But your goal should be to build a loyal customer base that connects with you on an emotional level. You can only achieve that by being open and transparent about what's important to you.

Remember though, if you talk about your values, you have to walk the walk also. Potential customers will check you out to see if you really do business according to your values. That's another opportunity for you—show them that you mean what you say, and you'll build another layer of trust with them!

To achieve long-term success, you must understand the priorities that virtually all high achievers make routine habits. Connect with these priorities and try to make them so second-nature that they are always operating in the background of everything you do.

We believe the following 3 priorities can literally make you unstoppable, if you choose to embrace them. They are:

★ **Self-discipline:** Self-discipline, in this context, means a number of things. It means that once you start something, you finish it. You resist the bright shiny object syndrome that afflicts so many entrepreneurs; creating sustained momentum is very difficult if you are easily distracted.

Self-discipline also means that you pursue excellence in everything you or your company does. The entrepreneurial lifestyle won't work for you if mediocre is good enough in your book. Committing to excellence builds customer loyalty, attracts world-class team members and differentiates you in the marketplace.

At its core, self-discipline means making decisions based on what's right; not what feels good at the moment. The right decisions benefit your clients/customers, your team and honor your vision and values instead of surrendering to expediency and convenience. Self-disciplined leaders make conscious, deliberate decisions and avoid cutting corners or compromising principles to squeeze a few extra dollars from a transaction.

★ **Tenacity:** Tenacity is simply not giving up, no matter the circumstance. Tenacity is refusing to allow opposition, uncertainty and the occasional failure stop you. Any time you move forward and upset the status quo, you will likely face adversity. The question is: What will you do about it?

When you encounter opposition, failure or adversity, you have two options. You can quit, which is always the wrong option; or you can regroup, learn from your mistakes, and move forward. Unfortunately, many entrepreneurs throw in the towel the very first time they run into a real challenge. We strongly believe tenacity sets most MVEs apart from other entrepreneurs, since we understand that adversity and temporary failure makes us stronger. Never give up and never surrender!

★ **Commitment to self-development:** The skills and knowledge required to successfully navigate business start-ups are not the same skills you will need to take the business to the next level. In truth, if you are not continuously growing as a leader, you will eventually stifle your company's success. Don't be the anchor or lodestone that weighs the company down: set the example through continuous learning and growth.

How do you keep growing as a leader? You have many options. Commit to reading a certain number of leadership/business books per year. Go to leadership seminars and boot camps. Pursue a professional designation that is noteworthy in your industry. In reality, exactly how you do it is less important than your commitment to doing it!

Investing in coaching and mastermind groups are two of the best ways to enhance your skills. Find a coach who understands where you need to go as a leader, and can help you get there. A good mastermind group will enable you to grow, think and stretch. You will find that the money you invest in these programs is money well spent, since you are investing in your most valuable business asset—you!

One final priority we strongly suggest you establish in your business from day one is uncompromising ethics. We encourage you to set and maintain the highest possible ethical standards for both yourself and your company. The commitment to ethics is so important we dedicate the next section to a detailed discussion.

Choose the harder right over the easier wrong.
—West Point maxim

Maintain Your Moral Compass

Not long ago, Time magazine declared the first decade of the 21st century as the "Decade from Hell." How did they come to this conclusion? One key factor was the extensive financial upheaval and corruption prevalent during the decade. Think Enron, WorldCom, the dot-com boom and bust, Lehmann Brothers, Bernie Madoff and a whole host of similar sordid characters. There are literally dozens of examples during this time period of people taking ethical shortcuts to obtain short term success, often ruining hundreds or thousands of lives in the process.

Of course, the media and popular culture feeds right into the perception that all business owners are crooks out for a quick profit at another's expense. In movies, business leaders are typically portrayed as one-dimensional villains, looking to make money by any means available, legal or illegal.

In movies, business leaders are typically portrayed as one-dimensional villains...

In reality, business people who fit that description are quite rare. Most business owners care deeply about their customers. They care about their employees. They are very involved in their communities and their families. Unfortunately, those villain stereotypes still persist. A tiny fraction of unscrupulous business leaders allow their low ethical standards to taint the reputation of the vast majority of honest, hard-working business leaders.

Based on our research and experience many, if not most, of these disgraced business leaders started off as basically honest people. At some point though, they chose to cut corners. Maybe they told a little white lie to a client to close a deal. Perhaps they took credit for something they didn't do, to get a promotion they didn't deserve. Ethical lapses usually start small and then grow until they take over the life of the person committing them.

The best way to keep from going down that road is to set your moral and ethical standards at the very beginning of your career. You must decide from the start that you won't cut corners, no matter what.

This is where your ethical standards tie into the self-discipline we mentioned in the last section. You cannot make decisions based on how you feel in the moment or what's expedient. In the heat of the battle, you might feel like throwing ethics out the window in order to make a quick sale, especially if your business is having a really tight month. You must decide beforehand that you will always occupy the highest moral ground.

The truth is, if you do stick to the highest moral standards, people won't always understand what you are doing. Some business peers may even think you are foolish because you don't pad your invoices or undercut your competition with artificially low bids. Doing what's right isn't always popular.

You need to establish the highest ethical standards for your team members also. Stress the values important to your company, even during the interview process. The best time to weed out people who don't share your ethical standards is before you hire them. If you find that one of your team members cuts ethical corners, even in minor areas, don't ignore it, look the other way and hope things will straighten themselves out. They won't! Deal with the situation swiftly and decisively.

It's difficult to discipline or even terminate an employee, especially one who makes money for the company. Minor ethical lapses are dangerous for a number of reasons. One reason is that a team member who will lie to, or cheat a customer in order to gain an advantage will do the same to you. You may profit from this employee's misdeeds at first, but cleaning up their mess will cost you far more in the long run.

The cost involved with ethical lapses isn't purely financial, although it may include money. The costs can involve lost customers, lawsuits, and most importantly, respect. When you lose the respect of your customers and peers, it's difficult (if not impossible) to get it back. It's far too high a price to pay just to make a quick buck.

To achieve enduring success, you must build on the foundation of the highest ethical standards. People, customers and team members alike, want to attach themselves to a company that's clear about what it stands for, and does what it says it will do. Unfortunately, there aren't many companies that strive to maintain those standards, so you will stand out in your industry!

In the next section, we share our most important reason to always act ethically. Now more than any other time in history, you have the opportunity to affect countless lives with your actions. It's time to ask yourself the question: What will my legacy be?

Leaving A Legacy Of Significance

How do you want people to remember you? It's a question you may not have given much thought. After all, we vetrepreneurs are doers, not philosophers. That said, it is important to put some thought into your legacy, into the effect you are having on the world around you and the imprint you will leave behind when you die.

When we talk about leaving a legacy, many MVEs think about the tangible assets we leave behind. In reality, there's far more to a legacy than money, investments and property. Your legacy is the impact you had on the people your life touched. You don't begin building a legacy just before you die. You begin your legacy long before your final days. In the very beginning of this book, we suggested beginning with the end in mind. This is partly what we meant, you should build your legacy as you build your entrepreneurial career.

Your legacy is the impact you had on the people your life touched

How many people will you actually touch in your lifetime? Far more than you probably think. Your "Sphere of Influence" includes everyone you touch as you go through life. You have the ability to affect the lives of everyone in your Sphere of Influence, either positively or negatively. Of course, that includes your family and friends. It also includes your vendors, your employees, your customers and your neighbors.

★ ★ ★ ★ ★ ★ ★ ★ ★ ★ ★ ★ ★ ★ ★ ★

Intel Insight

Your Sphere of Influence

The world gets smaller every day. We are more interconnected than ever, with more people taking advantage of the possibilities afforded to us by social networking. What does that mean to an MVE? Many things, especially in terms of marketing and staying connected to your clients/customers.

But we want you to think right now in terms of your Sphere of Influence. The fact that we can connect with more people means that our reach is longer than it has ever been. You can touch the lives of people across the planet—people you may never meet in person! It's time to start asking yourself: How will I use this new interconnectedness to positively impact people's lives? How can I use social media, and other tools, to make a difference?

You may be wondering just how big your Sphere of Influence is. Several years ago, Larry ran some numbers to find out and a conservative estimate yielded over 200,000—a number that has undoubtedly grown since then. Even if you own a very small business, your Sphere of Influence could easily number in the thousands. Don't sell yourself short... you probably have a much broader reach than you think!

If you operate your business and your life by pursuing excellence and the highest ethical standards, your Sphere of Influence is going to be positively affected. But if you start cheating people and your business goes under, many people will be negatively affected. You should find that extremely motivating. You can positively affect hundreds, if not thousands, of people simply by sticking to your vision and values.

One of the best ways we know for a person to start thinking about their legacy is to consider their own funeral. It may sound a little morbid, but think about these questions: What do you want people to say about you after you die? What do you want your family to say? What about your team members, or your business competitors? Which charities will show their appreciation because of your contributions?

It's sobering to think in these terms, but we believe it's the best way to get you to concentrate on the kind of life you want to live.

Once you visualize what you want to happen, it's time to take the next step. Decide what you need to do in order to build the legacy you visualized when you thought of your own funeral. Begin building that life today, so that when the end of your life comes, your legacy will be assured.

> *Few men during their lifetime come anywhere near*
> *exhausting the resources dwelling within them.*
> *There are deep wells of strength that are never used.*
> —*Admiral Richard Byrd*

Million Dollar Minute

We talked about this in the last section; now we want you to do it. Take a few minutes to write your own obituary. Assume that you lived to a ripe old age and write about the most important aspects of your life, as they relate to your business. What was most important to you? Whose life did you pour yourself into? What did your business achieve in the community, and in the world at large?

Remember, this obituary should represent what you want to be true at the end of your life. Think about what you want to have achieved, and who you made an impact on. What will your legacy to be?

DEVELOPING YOUR VICTORY SUCCESS PLAN

★ ★ ★ ★ ★ ★ ★ ★ ★ ★ ★ ★ ★ ★ ★ ★ ★ ★

There is no substitute for victory.
—Douglas MacArthur

We've covered a lot of ground in this book, from Vision to Team and from Intel to OPS. We've asked you to complete the *StrengthsFinder 2.0* and *Kolbe A Index* assessments to empower you to know yourself better and to become a more effective entrepreneur and leader. We've strongly suggested you reach out and create a service-based relationship with a mentor and/or hire a coach. We've challenged you to complete the **Million Dollar Minute** exercises and break free from the inertia that's keeping you stuck.

So…have you done any of it? Have you taken action on anything? Have you implemented even one thing in this book, or have you absorbed all the information, filed it away and told yourself, "I'll get to that tomorrow?"

If you've stepped up and done even one thing, especially something that took you out of your comfort zone, bravo! If you haven't, then we suggest you pass this book on to another vetrepreneur who will actually do something with it, or just throw it in your recycling bin. Why? Because you're probably not cut out to be an MVE.

Now, there's nothing wrong with that, and just the fact that you picked up this book and read it definitely says something about you. You simply may not be ready yet. You may need to hone your skills and confidence working for someone else for a while. That's fine and we applaud you for recognizing that and making a conscious decision NOT to jump into the entrepreneurial pool with your hands and feet tied. Put this book on your bookshelf, within easy reach, so you can see the spine and re-read sections that really speak to you as you progress through your career. One day, when you're ready, it will be time.

Maybe connecting with what it REALLY takes to successfully navigate self-employment created a gnawing fear in your stomach you can't overcome. No sweat…you likely have some great skills and will make a great employee within someone else's company. In fact, just approaching your job with the vetrepreneur mindset we've laid out in this book will help you stand head and shoulders above the vast majority of your fellow employees. Treating employment as if it were your own business can lead to rapid advancement and significant contributions to your company, your family and your community.

We've stated it throughout this book: The KEY test that separates highly successful vetrepreneurs from those who limp along in mediocrity or completely fail, is taking rapid, decisive action. If you made it all the way through this book and did nothing, you failed (and failed badly). Did we just piss you off? Good!

If you're still serious about being a real MVE, clear an hour from your schedule RIGHT NOW and use the outline below to immediately start crafting your VICTORY Success Plan. If not, if our challenge still hasn't created even a tiny amount of forward momentum, that's fine. We part ways as friends and we wish you the very best!

STOP READING! To accomplish this, you will need a notebook/ journal/scratch paper, your electronic or paper calendar, your favorite pen and a big red marker. Optional accessories include good thinking music and your favorite adult beverage (or two). Now lock the doors, send the kids to Grandma's and give your spouse the credit card. Check your watch, write down the time and get going…your hour has started!

Your VICTORY Success Action Plan

VISION

★ Take 5 minutes and write out your company vision statement. Don't self-edit, just let it flow.

★ Take 5 minutes and write out your personal vision statement. As above, don't self-edit. Clearly state the income, lifestyle, accomplishments and community impact you desire. Put it on paper.

★ Read each of these back 3 times with as much energy and gusto as you can muster. Don't be timid, declare out loud what you are all about!

INTEL

★ Take 5 minutes and write down the 3 pieces of specific information you don't know right now that are holding you back from making sales, landing the contract you're after, hiring the right team.

★ Take 2 minutes and write down one immediate step you can take in the next 24 hours to gain clarity for each piece of Intel. Don't discard ideas as silly or irrelevant…your first, gut response is usually the one you should go with!

COACHING

★ Set the kitchen timer for 3 minutes and make a list of every single center of influence you can think of in your industry (or industry you want to break into). Try to get at least 10.

★ Take another 2 minutes and choose the top three from that list.

★ Set up a "Google Alert" for each name. Over the next 2 weeks, check the alerts daily and any time one of these three is referenced in an article, interview, business accomplishment, send a handwritten congratulatory note. In the third note, ask for 10 minutes of the their time for a short information call (you'll be amazed at how many say "yes"). This shouldn't take more than 5 minutes.

★ Don't know how to set a Google Alert? Google it…

TEAM

★ Dust off your 3-column exercise and find the one task or item on the list that makes your skin crawl or stomach knot up. Circle it in red (this should take no more than 30 seconds).

★ Make outsourcing, delegating or deleting this task your TOP priority on your To Do list.

★ You'll need 30 minutes to figure out how to make this happen—schedule the 30-minute block on your calendar right now to complete within the next 12 hours.

★ You now have 48 hours from the time you make the calendar entry to make this a reality. After you get rid of the first thing, the others become much easier!

OPS

★ Imagine a truck hits you precisely at 0817 tomorrow morning. Ouch! The good news? You're not dead. The bad news? You won't be able to do ANYTHING in your business for the next week.

★ Take 5 minutes and write down the top three critical processes or systems that would completely fall apart after your close encounter with the angry truck. Don't BS yourself...write 'em down.

★ Choose the Number 1 most critical system and circle it with your red marker. Put a 1-hour appointment on your calendar for sometime within the next 24 hours, get on some sort of recording device and regurgitate EVERYTHING you can think of about the right way (i.e., your way) of handling this system. Don't skimp on the details. It should be complete enough that a 15-year old could listen to it and get it 75 percent right.

★ Complete this process with all three top systems in the next 48 hours and get all 3 recordings transcribed. Congrats! You have the beginning of your customized OPS Manual (visit our web resources at **www.VictorySuccessResources.com** if you need help making this happen).

RAPID ACTION

★ Take 3 minutes and write down every single thought or idea you have swirling around in your head right now. If you've actually done everything above...there are probably 25 or more.

★ Grab your red marker and take 1 minute to scroll down the list. Circle the first 2 items that jump off the page at you. Don't think about it...just do it.

★ Schedule 15 minutes of time for each item (30 minutes total) on your calendar RIGHT NOW to do within the next 24 hours... spend that time thinking, doodling and jotting down everything you can think of about that item.

★ They popped out for a reason, so chances are they are something you need to act on immediately. Don't spend time second-guessing yourself, just get into action!

YOU

★ You should be right at the 45-minute mark and we have reserved the most time to focus on your most important business asset.

★ Take a clean sheet of paper, take 5 minutes total and write down one specific business goal and one specific personal goal for the next 12 months. Don't be a wuss...we aren't looking for a "run of the mill" SMART (Specific, Measurable, Achievable, Realistic and Timeframe) Goal, we are looking for B-HAGs (Big Hairy Audacious Goals).

★ If something immediately pops in your mind and your inner critic committee starts screaming about how it can't be done, send them to the woodshed and write it down anyway.

★ Spend 5 minutes simply connecting with these goals and think about who you want to be to achieve these goals (not necessarily what you need to do). Think about the values and principles you will embody and what accomplishing them will feel like. Step into how awesome accomplishing these goals will be.

★ Take your remaining time (3-5 minutes) and complete this declaration:

> *It's* _____ *(date 1 year from today) and it has been the most incredible year! In my business, I accomplished* _____ *and in my personal life, I accomplished* _____ *. I am proud and excited and thankful.*

Now stop, put down your pen, lean back and take a sip of that favorite beverage…

Congratulations! You just accomplished more strategic planning in a single hour than many entrepreneurs will do all year. Wasn't that hard, was it? Religiously and consciously do this every one to two weeks and you will become an unstoppable entrepreneurial force, regardless of your industry. The three simple keys to making this work time and again are:

★ Schedule 1 hour a week; put it on the calendar and make it sacrosanct.
★ Don't over think it, move fast and don't look back. Write down the first thing that comes to mind and don't second guess it.
★ This process will flush out your inner critics and gremlins. They will scream, cry, throw things and make every effort to erase the bold and replace it with the old, tired story. Tell them to pound sand and send them to the corner.

That's it…it doesn't need to be any more complicated than this. You're now well on your way, and we are really excited for your. Your VICTORY Success Plan will have a big impact in your industry, your community, your family and your life. Finally, drop us a line at

Success@VictorySuccessSystem.com and share your results for this exercise…we would love to hear them and promise they will stay confidential.

> *Cowardice is almost always simply the lack of ability to suspend the functioning of the imagination.*
> —*Ernest Hemingway*
> *Ambulance Driver, WWI*
> *Reporter in the Spanish Civil War*
> *European Combat Correspondent WWII*

FREEDOM ROAD

★ ★ ★ ★ ★ ★ ★ ★ ★ ★ ★ ★ ★ ★ ★ ★ ★ ★

I offer neither pay, nor quarters, nor food: I offer only hunger, thirst,
forced marches, battles and death. Let him who loves his country
with his heart, and not merely his lips, follow me.
—*Giuseppe Garibaldi, Italian patriot and soldier*

A Crisis of Leadership

Over the past few decades, we've witnessed multiple scandals in virtually every area of our society: political, financial, religious and social. We are witnessing the mortgaging our children's and our grandchildren's future by short-sighted politicians who use the labor of the productive to buy the votes of the ever increasing dependency class. They're spending staggering sums bailing out individuals, companies and quasi-government organizations for bad decisions and poor behavior with virtually no accountability or regard for our national fiscal state.

Further, we are experiencing an unprecedented leadership vacuum from the halls of Washington, D.C. to corporate boardrooms to state capitols and beyond. The political elites and the 24/7 news cycle "yammering" class of professional pontificators are far more concerned about being right than doing what's right. Cocooned within the detached fantasyland inside the DC Beltway, they increasingly view the 70 percent of Americans who work hard, raise their children, pay their taxes and mortgages and want only to create a comfortable life, as little more than serfs.

They compound this view by putting every imaginable barrier in front of those willing to step up and start businesses; from mind numbingly bizarre regulatory webs to ridiculous employment rules to a confusing labyrinth of confiscatory taxes. Their "mini-mes" in a significant number of state legislatures followed suit, resulting in incredibly hostile business environments, especially for start-ups, in many states. Finally, they are abetted by a small, but powerful group of corporate "bad apples" that seek to protect market share, profits and multi-million dollar bonuses by underwriting ever-increasing barriers to entry for new entrepreneurs.

The net result? Crippling job losses, stubbornly high unemployment (especially among military veterans), a growing national security risk as we slide from super-power to debtor nation, and a generation of Americans in what should be their peak earning years convinced their children will inherit a land of fewer freedoms and far less opportunity. This is exactly why we need YOU!

Are you Ready to Take Point?

We need you to step up and lead. Now, perhaps more than at any other time in our history, America needs its military veterans, and MVEs in particular, to "take point" in our communities, business circles and even elective offices. We need forward-thinking men and women of action dedicated to upholding the highest standards of conduct, values and service that make this country great to stand up and be heard.

We cannot allow the ethical capitulation of our country to continue unchallenged. We may not be able to stem the tide in every area. But in the activities we involve ourselves in, especially our businesses, our families and our communities, we can show our fellow Americans what honor, duty and service look like. We believe MVEs are perfectly suited to stand in the breach and confront these enormous economic and societal challenges. We've already served once, putting our lives on the line defending this great nation and we are imploring you to step forward, join us and become part of the solution…part of the Vetrepreneur Revolution!

The Vetrepreneur Revolution

We firmly believe that entrepreneurship is the clearest path to economic freedom, self-determination and creating a lasting legacy. Notice we didn't say easiest path, the road can be tough, but you're tougher! We also believe MVEs represent enormous potential for positive economic and societal change. We have the power to create our own economic stimulus for our families, our communities, our nation and ourselves.

We can reach out and employ fellow veterans as our businesses grow, paying it forward. We can lead the ethical charge by refusing to compromise our principles and values and asking others to do the same. We can become a driving force in lifting our country out of this crisis mindset and placing it firmly on the road to freedom once more.

We are dedicating the balance of our professional lives to raising and advancing this banner. We humbly ask you to step forward, join us and take up the call. Lock n' load…we're moving out!

The Entrepreneur's Creed

I do not choose to be a common man. It is my right to be uncommon—if I can. I seek opportunity—not security. I do not wish to be a kept citizen, humbled and dulled by having the state look after me. I want to take the calculated risk, to dream and to build, to fail and to succeed. I refuse to barter incentive for a dole; I prefer the challenges of life to the guaranteed existence: the thrill of fulfillment to the stale calm of Utopia. I will not trade my freedom for beneficence, nor my dignity for a handout. I will never cower before any earthly master nor bend to any threat. It is my heritage to stand erect, proud and unafraid: to think and act for myself, to enjoy the benefit of my creations and to face the world boldly and say: "This, with God's help I have done." All this is what it means to be an entrepreneur.

Author Unknown

In the Arena

It is not the critic who counts; not the man who points out how the strong man stumbles, or where the doer of deeds could have done them better. The credit belongs to the man who is actually in the arena, whose face is marred by dust and sweat and blood; who strives valiantly; who errs, comes up short again and again, because there is no effort without error and shortcoming; but who does actually strive to do the deeds; who knows the great enthusiasms, the great devotions; who spends himself in a worthy cause; who at the best knows in the end the triumph of high achievement, and who at the worst, if he fails, at least fails while daring greatly, so that his place shall never be with those cold and timid souls who neither know victory nor defeat.

President Theodore Roosevelt
Speech at the Sorbonne
Paris, France
April 23, 1910

RESOURCES

★ ★

We were going to provide dozens of pages of top resources in this section and then came to our senses!

Since new resources become available all the time, we decided to spare some trees and invite you to visit:

www.VictorySuccessResources.com

You will find the latest resources for:

★ Coaching
★ Marketing
★ Outsourcing
★ Team Building
★ Business Systems
★ Inspiration and Motivation
★ Supporting Fellow Veterans
★ Government Support Programs
★ and much, much more

LEARN MORE

★ ★ ★ ★ ★ ★ ★ ★ ★ ★ ★ ★ ★ ★ ★ ★ ★ ★ ★ ★

Thank you for taking the time to read this book, and thank you for your service to our country. We know from personal experience the lifetime value of just one powerful idea or mindset shift. Our B-HAG was connecting you with two or three ideas, resources or strategies you can immediately implement to improve your business (or initial business plan, if you are just getting started). Honestly, if we simply connected you with that ONE idea or shift, then we have accomplished our mission and would love to hear about it at **Success@VictorySuccessSystem.com**.

We believe in you—our fellow vetrepreneurs. You are the sole reason we wrote this book. We are passionate about helping you build the business you desire and creating the life you deserve. We want to support you in making a positive impact on your clients/customers, your community and your family. We've been blessed to connect with incredible coaches and mentors as we've grown our respective businesses and we are serious about paying it forward!

We invite you to use the touch-points below to stay connected. Use them to celebrate your triumphs, learn from your failures, and to voice your frustrations or challenges from a place of openness and curiosity, so other MVEs facing similar obstacles realize they aren't alone. Together we can explore solutions that benefit all of us!

Finally, we would like to share our B-HAG (Big Hairy Audacious Goal): We aspire to awaken the enormous latent power for ethical business success within the MVE community. We seek to inspire fellow vetrepreneurs to step forward, "take point" and provide leadership at every level in our society. In short, we are raising the positive standard of the Vetrepreneur Revolution and invite you to join us!

Staying Connected

www.VictorySuccessSystem.com: Visit our web base for the latest information on:

★ Cutting edge vetrepreneur tools.
★ Success stories from fellow MVEs.
★ Video, audio and print interviews with top national vetrepreneurs.
★ Access to mission-tested resources to grow your business and build your team.
★ Special "Web Only Bonuses" for purchasers of this book.

Coaching with Larry and Phil: One of the fastest ways to create sustained positive momentum in your business is hiring the right coach. We know this from intimate personal experience. We continue to invest heavily each year in top coaches and fully credit our coaches and mentors as catalysts for our continued success.

Each year, we work with a limited number of MVEs who are serious about making quantum leaps in their business. We have over 60 years of proven entrepreneurial and leadership success under our belt, and have coached dozens of entrepreneurs and business owners to new heights. We offer several ways to work with us, including:

* **VICTORY Success Circle:** Membership in this high-value, low-investment program entitles you to our monthly success tips delivered right to your in-box, our monthly interview with top vetreprenurs and experts in a variety of business building areas, and member-only bonuses/discounts in a password protected portion of our web base.

* **Rapid Results Strategy Session:** This laser-focus 45-minute phone strategy session is perfect to help you break through a specific obstacle or receive timely guidance around a key opportunity. SPECIAL BONUS: We record and transcribe the call for your on-going reference.

* **Fireteam Mastermind®:** This high-power 6-month mastermind program combines a powerful mix of individual phone strategy calls with team mastermind phone coaching calls for 8-10 vetrepreneurs committed to excellence. You will experience significant business breakthroughs and forward acceleration through this robust channel. SPECIAL BONUSES: All individual and group calls are recorded and transcribed. Fireteam members also receive complimentary access to the VICTORY Success Circle during their program and a special discount on Elite VIP Strategy Days.

* **Elite VIP Strategy Day:** For vetrepreneurs truly ready to make a quantum leap in their business, we offer a very limited number of Elite VIP Strategy Days in Los Angeles, CA or Baltimore, MD with Larry and Phil. You receive live 2-on-1 coaching that routinely generates 6-figure plus business ideas and is the equivalent of 6-12 months of coaching in a single day. You will leave with a detailed 90-day Action Plan to implement your breakthroughs. SPECIAL BONUSES: All Elite VIP coaching members receive private 90-minute pre- and post-VIP day strategy calls, complimentary

membership on a Fireteam Mastermind® and complimentary access to the VICTORY Success Circle.

★ Visit **www.VictorySuccessCoaching.com** for more information.

★ **Live Events:** We believe one of the best ways to create breakthroughs in your business is to network with other top achievers. We have developed several live event formats designed to both deliver the latest business building information and connect you with top vetrepreneurs and resources around the country. A full list of our live events is located at **www.VictorySuccessEvents.com.**

THE AUTHORS

★ ★ ★ ★ ★ ★ ★ ★ ★ ★ ★ ★ ★ ★ ★ ★ ★ ★ ★

Larry Broughton:
Co-Founder of the VICTORY Success System, award-winning entrepreneur, author, speaker and family guy. After growing up in a small mill town in rural New York, he spent eight years with the US Army's elite Special Forces, commonly known as the Green Berets. During this time, he traveled extensively around the world and attained the rank of Staff Sergeant.

Larry has parlayed his unique experience of serving on Special Forces A-Teams to the business world. He is Founder/CEO of Broughton Hospitality. Since its inception, his firm has received numerous awards for performance, and is considered a leader in the boutique hotel industry. He has been awarded Ernst & Young's prestigious Entrepreneur of the Year Award® and the National Veteran-Owned Business Association named him their Vetrepreneur® of the Year, while *Entrepreneur Magazine* named his firm among their Hot 500 Fastest Growing Privately Held Companies.

Larry's upbeat, creative approach to business has been featured in articles from the *Los Angeles Times* and *New York Times* to *Entrepreneur Magazine*; on dozens of national radio shows, and on every major television network.

Larry is the co-author of *The Next Big Thing: Top Trends to Dominate the New Economy*; and author of *FLASHPOINTS For Achievers*, and *Green Beret Lessons On Leadership*. He is a popular keynote speaker on the topics of leadership, entrepreneurship, and veterans causes.

Larry lives in Irvine, CA with his bride, Suzanne; their daughter, Emily; and son, Ben.

Phil Dyer:
Co-Founder of the VICTORY Success System, West Point graduate, and former Army Captain. Commissioned into the Armor Branch, he was stationed with 1/32 and 4/67 Armor ("Bandits"), 3AD in Friedberg, Germany. After serving on active duty, Phil enjoyed highly successful "duty assignments" in corporate sales for a Fortune 50 company, as a fee-only financial planner and as a national financial educator for a major military association.

Over the last 15 years, Phil has counseled hundreds of entrepreneurs and thousands of transitioning military service members on financial, tax and success strategies. He has given over 675 speeches on a broad variety of financial/business topics and has shared the stage with some of today's most innovative business thought leaders.

A prolific writer and author, Phil has over 100 business/financial by-lines in major magazines and is frequently quoted in publications such as *Money, Kiplinger's, Men's Health* and many others. He is the co-author of *VICTORY: 7 Entrepreneur Success Strategies for Veterans* with Larry Broughton (January 2011) and the forthcoming *Conscious Business Revolution* with Jessica Eaves Mathews (March 2011). He is also author of the forthcoming *Dream Big. Start Small. Move Fast: The 9 New Entrepreneur Success Strategies.*

A serial entrepreneur, Phil has run and sold two small businesses and currently actively owns a boutique financial planning practice and a strategic consulting business. 300 small business peers recently recognized him with their MVC (Most Valuable Contributor) award marketing and business building innovations.

Phil loves visiting Tuscany, Italian wine, adventure travel and spending time with his wife and children in Baldwin, MD.